$8⁰⁰

D0096184

SURVIVING THE DEBT STORM
GETTING CAPITALISM BACK ON TRACK

SURVIVING THE DEBT STORM
GETTING CAPITALISM BACK ON TRACK

Leigh Skene and Melissa Kidd

P
PROFILE BOOKS

First published in Great Britain in 2013 by
Profile Books Ltd
3A Exmouth House
Pine Street
London EC1R 0JH
www.profilebooks.com

Copyright © Lombard Street Research 2013

The moral right of the authors has been asserted.

All rights reserved. Without limiting the rights under copyright reserved above, no part
of this publication may be reproduced, stored or introduced into a retrieval system,
or transmitted, in any form or by any means (electronic, mechanical, photocopying,
recording or otherwise), without the prior written permission of both the copyright
owner and the publisher of this book.

Typeset in Times by MacGuru Ltd
info@macguru.org.uk
Printed and bound in Britain by
Bell & Bain Ltd

A CIP catalogue record for this book is available from the British Library.

ISBN 978 1 78125 105 8
eISBN 978 1 84765 952 1

MIX
Paper from
responsible sources
FSC® C007785

Contents

Figures and tables

Acknowledgements

I wish to thank the many people who contributed their knowledge and skills to making *Surviving the Debt Storm: Getting Capitalism Back on Track* the fine publication that it is. I thank Peter Allen, without whose nagging I would never started it: his enthusiasm for the project was vital in keeping it moving forward through its various stages. I thank Melissa for joining me as co-author, and for her help in defining the structure and objectives of the book and her cheerful acceptance of my, shall we say, bossy ways as we wrote it. I thank my wife Kathy for reading every word, more than once, and her suggestions for improving readability.

I thank Stephen Brough at Profile Books for supporting our vision and his pithy comments on how to refine it. I thank the staff of Profile for their invaluable help in creating a book that Melissa and I are proud of. Finally, I thank Anthony Hilton and Jamil Baz for reviewing the book and finding some kind words to say about it.

Leigh Skene

Introduction

October 24th 2019, the 90th anniversary of the Wall Street Crash, is the third anniversary of the even worse Great Default – the day when a bank too big to fail proved to be too big to bail out. Its failure triggered a chain reaction of defaults that collapsed the Ponzi scheme of insolvent banks supporting the insolvent governments that guaranteed the liabilities of the insolvent banks. Public and private defaults combined to slash money supplies in OECD countries and the consequent soaring real interest rates decimated stock, commodity, precious metals and housing prices and caused the deepest depression in recorded history throughout Europe and North America.

Banking system collapses have annihilated credit markets and even the few borrowers with investment-grade credit ratings cannot borrow. Conditions are worse than when the monetary system collapsed in 1931. Government revenue streams have shrunk to a trickle and services have shrivelled commensurately. Benefits are virtually non-existent, so civil disobedience and violence continue to rise. Developed countries' great expectations for emerging country growth to provide export markets vanished, with China plummeting into prolonged recession. Instead, China is trying to distract its increasingly restive population from their problems with an aggressive foreign policy that has now caused a naval clash with the US Seventh Fleet in the South China Sea and …

Can this actually happen?

Indeed it can! This book is a searing indictment of banks and the agenda that has been adopted by governments and central banks. It makes the compelling case that, because of the gargantuan efforts to derail the deleverage that is inevitable after the collapse of the greatest credit bubble of all time, the authorities have placed themselves in the middle of a 'damned if they do and damned if they don't' situation that will ultimately result in a considerably more painful correction of global and national imbalances than necessary. At its worst, the unfolding of this crisis could feature:

- bank failures and nationalisation of financial institutions and significant shortages of the capital needed to recapitalise banks;
- sovereign, non-financial corporate and household defaults;
- falling global savings and rising global real interest rates;
- plummeting asset prices – stocks, bonds, housing, commodities, precious metals, etc;
- dysfunctional capital markets;
- falling money supplies, in spite of massive money printing, causing lower real incomes and negative output growth in developed countries;
- central banks financing massive government deficits;
- higher taxes and reduced government services and benefits;
- exits from the euro;
- a sharp drop in China's trend growth rate with bank recapitalisations and weak yuan.

Yet it is still not too late to choose a different path.

Implementing the hubristic hypothesis that fiscal and monetary policy can always avoid boom-and-bust has placed developed countries firmly in the path of the greatest bust of all time. This book will show that we created the biggest credit bubble of all time by ignoring the lessons past crises had taught. It goes on to show how all the favourable conditions that helped recovery from past crises have turned unfavourable and explains how the euro-zone crisis compares with past events. It then shows how unwarranted fear of deflation has resulted in policies that have been counterproductive, and describes policies that could help correct imbalances and the restructuring that is necessary to return to optimal growth and robust financial markets. In short, it explains what we need to do to get from where we are to where we want to be.

1

Why bubbles? Why do they always burst?

Economic theory assumes all people know all the relevant facts concerning all their economic decisions and always act rationally on the information – 'rational man'. The efficient markets hypothesis asserts that financial markets embody all the information that can affect prices. If so, consistently achieving above-average market-risk-adjusted returns would be impossible and the entire industry devoted to financial analysis would be superfluous. Nevertheless, 'rational man' + efficient markets = predictability, so mathematical computer models based on these assumptions have proliferated. Blind faith in their ability to predict the future with decimal-point accuracy, to price complicated asset structures correctly and to accurately identify all possible sources of risk led to an explosion in the amount of debt outstanding and rapidly rising leverage up to the financial crisis in 2008–09.

'Rational man' does not exist – and never did. Desires and fears, i.e. emotions, drive all human activity. They are neither rational nor linear, so they cannot be modelled. However, they do fluctuate within given parameters – most of the time. Resulting behaviours can be modelled as long as the emotions stay within the parameters and historical relationships continue. This is a big ask and gives rise to another three problems that bedevil model predictions. First, extreme events pop up far more frequently than mathematical theory predicts. Second, models cannot predict when an extreme event will occur. Third, they cannot give any reliable information on an extreme event – even after it has occurred – so the models still cannot incorporate the effects of the end of over half a century of ever-increasing leverage on economies and financial markets.

Furthermore, many analysts ignore financial debt when computing debt-to-GDP ratios – odd, because excess financial debt always causes or exacerbates financial crises. Financial debt in the US fell 20% from its high at the end of 2008 while rising 10% in Europe, so the next banking crisis should start in Europe, where the creditworthiness of sovereign debt has fallen alarmingly in some of the peripheral states.[1] Moreover, bankers on both sides of the Atlantic are continuing to make two serious errors that were major factors in the banking crisis of 2007–8:

• putting more reliance on computer models than on common sense;
• failing to purge bank balance sheets of failing assets due to inadequate net tangible equity to absorb the losses.

Contrary to the hype, computer models are highly fallible. (Remember 'garbage in = garbage out'?) They greatly underestimated financial risk by failing to incorporate obvious correlations and, for example, rated securities based on home equity loans and subprime mortgages AAA. Reliance on computer models also explains the failure to spot turning points. Only external shocks can divert models from moving towards equilibrium. All computer-driven forecasts tend to be straight lines towards equilibrium positions. Computer models do not, and probably never will, identify turning points.

Failure to adequately price complex financial instruments, especially collateralised debt obligations (CDOs), was a major factor in the 2007–08 subprime crisis. Securitisation effectively hedged the specific factors leading to default, such as personal illness, but failed completely to address the risks common to the entire securitised pool, such as an economic downturn and rising unemployment. Investors in the euro zone mispriced sovereign debt for a prolonged period of time, but for a different reason – the false assumption that a common monetary policy plus the political promise that no country in the region would default reduced sovereign risk within the euro.

Emotions exceeding known parameters cause extreme events, such as stock-market booms and busts. They are self-reinforcing spirals upward and especially downward that, once established, keep diverging from equilibrium until the driving forces fade or stronger counter-forces reverse them. Ever-increasing desires for accumulating ever-greater wealth faster and faster ignited a credit bubble that spiralled upwards until dwindling numbers of new borrowers burst the bubble in 2008. The multi-decade credit bubble and its bursting were extreme events. No model recognised the credit bubble for what it was, so could not predict its collapse. What is more, no model is giving any indication of the plethora of problems brewing in Europe.

Economists' inability to see self-reinforcing spirals has caused a long argument about whether the main cause of recessions and depressions is:

- an inherent tendency to overproduction within the capitalist economic system itself; or
- external shocks causing underconsumption.

The debate is unlikely to end because neither hypothesis is verifiable. This book will show that the main cause of recessions and depressions is that the interaction of human fear and greed produces recurrent cycles. However, distinguishing one cycle from another is hard. Cycles of different lengths and amplitudes interact, so they defy rigorous statistical analysis. By contrast, overproduction is only one aspect of human greed and shocks produce only random change. Consequently, analysis of underconsumption relies on abstract models that freeze all but a few variables to determine the effects of the remaining factors. Unfortunately, these models infer an equilibrium that exists only in theory and their adherents can always come up with factors to explain their failure to produce the predicted outcomes.

Both money and credit variables exhibit recurring long-term cycles. Repetitive behaviour underlies those cycles. As Mark Twain said, 'History does not repeat itself, but it does rhyme.' Rhyme creates repeating patterns that, over relatively consistent periods of time, constitute cycles. It is important to remember that cycles are not predetermined patterns, but the natural outcome of the inputs that have occurred. Charles Mackay initiated the discussion of credit cycles in his book *Extraordinary Popular Delusions and the Madness of Crowds*, first published in 1841. Present-day economists still refer to the three chapters on economic bubbles. Irving Fisher's theory of debt deflation advanced the study of credit cycles in 1933 by discovering the following sequence of eight events after credit bubbles burst, which causes a fall in nominal interest rates and a rise in real interest rates.

1 Contraction of the money supply and its velocity, as bank loans are paid off.
2 This debt liquidation causes distressed selling and
3 A fall in prices.
4 Assuming reflationary policies do not interfere with the fall in prices, there must be a still greater fall in the net worth of businesses, precipitating bankruptcies and
5 A likely fall in profits, which causes loss-making businesses to make
6 A reduction in output, in trade and in employment of labour, which leads to
7 Pessimism and loss of confidence, which in turn lead to
8 Hoarding and continual slowing of the velocity of circulation.

Hyman Minsky explained the evolution of credit cycles with his financial instability hypothesis in 1974. It identified three types of debt financing:

- Hedge – borrowers can pay principal and interest from income, so risk is minimal. Equity forms of finance predominate.
- Speculative – borrowers can pay interest from income, but need liquid financial markets to refinance the principal at maturity, so defaults rise when liquidity is impaired. Rollover risk can lead to refinancing crises and default of otherwise solvent companies.
- Ponzi – borrowers cannot pay either interest or principal out of income, so need the price of the asset to rise to service their debts. Defaults soar when asset prices stop rising because the stock of debt keeps rising as a percentage of assets.

Confidence (read greed) rises over a prolonged period of prosperity, so a capitalist economy moves from hedge finance dominating its financial structure to increasing domination by speculative and Ponzi finance. Financial markets and the economy are relatively stable when hedge financing dominates, but become ever more unstable as the proportions of speculative and Ponzi finance rise. The rising instability causes three debt corrections of increasing severity, which are described in detail in later chapters. The Penn Central Transportation Company default in 1970 caused the first correction in the US's current Minsky cycle. The 1989–90 savings and loan crisis caused the second and the Lehman Brothers/AIG default in 2008 caused the third. The start of the third correction is called a 'Minsky moment' and it initiates the self-reinforcing spiral downward that Fisher described.

The Minsky moment initiates a string of defaults and deflation that causes tightening lending standards until rising fear ensures hedge financing dominates once again. Such debt is self-liquidating and creates few, if any, problems, and so sets the stage for the next period of prolonged prosperity. Fisher and Minsky showed that credit cycles result from greed and fear interacting with the regulations designed to keep financial markets and the economy operating within reasonable bounds. External shocks neither cause cycles nor end them. Governments and central banks have all the fiscal and monetary policies they need to dampen credit cycles, popularly called boom-and-bust, forever. However, in an effort to fulfil their ambitions for perpetual above potential growth, they misused those policies and stimulated when economic conditions required tightening.

Debt was our most important product

In 1958 Merton Miller and Franco Modigliani espoused the theory that debt-to-equity ratios do not affect the value of companies – that is, leverage does not matter. Wrong – leverage does matter. However, wishful thinking extended this mistaken idea into the widespread belief that more credit can and will cure all economic and financial problems, so debt-to-GDP ratios soared. For example, the US total debt-to-GDP ratio is two-and-a-quarter times its level at the end of the Second World War. Excessive debt-to-GDP ratios are the main reason the recoveries in developed countries since the Great Recession cannot gain traction.

The function of debt is to transfer savings from savers to debtors, who can use the saving to create long-term assets. The interest paid on debt rewards savers for postponing consumption while debtors earn profits on their investments in excess of the interest on the debt. Natural rates of interest reward savers and debtors proportionately. Low profits decrease the demand for debt and interest rates fall until saving falls; high profits increase the demand for debt and interest rates rise until profits fall. The leads and lags inherent in the business cycle average out, so the incremental debt neither exceeds nor falls behind its proper proportion of saving for long. Incremental debt determines medium-term money supply growth, so natural rates of interest balance saving/investment and debt/money growth with economic growth over the course of a business cycle.

By contrast, excessive focus on GDP growth makes governments continuously pressurise central banks to hold interest rates below the natural rate. It takes a strong head of a central bank operating in a high and rising inflationary context to resist this pressure (see Chapter 3), so money and debt usually rise faster than saving and investment. The excess debt funds economic activity that otherwise would have occurred in the future, thereby reducing potential future economic activity until the debt is repaid. Incremental debt exceeding saving brings activity from the future to the present at ever-decreasing rates until important sectors can no longer pay the interest on their debt. The country has then reached its debt limit and the economy cannot respond to monetary stimulation. Debt limits vary among different economies and times. In 2012 they were about three-and-a-half times GDP in several developed countries.

The failure of fiscal and monetary stimulation to generate sustainable recoveries shows that many developed countries have run out of the ability to borrow from the future until they have repaid and/or defaulted on a sufficient amount of outstanding debt. Voluntary repayment causes much less turmoil than default because it reduces money and debt equally without hurting asset prices. Money balances fall but net worth (wealth) remains intact. By contrast, forced debt repayments and defaults reduce asset prices as well as money balances and debt, and so reduce wealth.

The double whammy of falling money balances and asset prices leaves the economy worse off than if the rise in the debt-to-GDP ratio had never occurred, so minimising forced debt repayment and defaults should be the first priority when debt problems arise. Borrowing more cannot solve the problem of too much debt, so credit should be cut off at the first sign of insolvency. Insolvent, but adequately liquid, borrowers can often work their way out of trouble by reducing their balance sheets. Even if they cannot, their defaults reduce wealth far less than when creditors keep pouring in good money after bad – as many developed countries and supranational agencies are now doing.

The main feature of running into debt limits is the chronic inability to produce adequate real growth. Japan reached that state in the 1990s and several countries including, but not limited to, the US, Spain, Italy, Greece, Portugal and Ireland reached it more recently, despite record fiscal and monetary stimulation. Higher unemployment, as a result of uncompetitive labour costs and a lack of new industries, is the main reason for this dismal performance. Many countries, especially in Europe, are trying to cure the problem of too much debt with more debt. They are sinking into depression – as are segments of society in others.

The error of choosing Miller and Modigliani over Fisher and Minsky is becoming clear. A Minsky moment minimises the ability to borrow from the future, ending the apparent ability of governments and central banks to control economic activity. That ability is apparent because they could only borrow from the future, and failure to repay the borrowing caused the Minsky moment. The Lehman/AIG default was the Minsky moment that ended the fifth major credit bubble. Government and central bank efforts since then have only made the ultimate outcome worse. The post-war credit bubble has indeed ended, despite government and central bank efforts to the contrary.

The first four Minsky credit cycles

Significant changes to credit availability greatly increase the amplitude of credit cycles. The resultant spectacular rises in the prices of assets and even more spectacular crashes affect financial markets for many years. Four such credit and asset price spirals and crashes occurred before the Second World War: tulip mania in the Dutch Republic in 1637; a British and French joint stock company bubble in 1720; a US real-estate bubble in 1837; and a US and European stock-market bubble that peaked in 1929. A fifth bubble, real estate in several countries, burst in 2007, but the resulting crash is not following the pattern of the preceding four. We will look at the first four cycles and the run-up to the 2007 peak and then discuss why this crash is different and how it is likely to play out.

A northward migration to escape Spanish rule brought a lot of capital into the Dutch Republic in the early 17th century. Banking began in the republic in 1609, which added credit to the capital inflow and set the stage for the first credit bubble. Tulips were rare and expensive – and so sought after. A lull in the Thirty Years War in the 1630s released money for frivolities and speculators began buying tulips. According to Morgan Stanley Research, tulip prices soared 5,900% in 36 months to a peak in 1637 and then crashed 93% in ten months. Even though this was one of the biggest asset bubbles ever, most tulips were bought with futures contracts that were never settled. This limited the amount of credit losses, so the negative impact of this first credit bubble was less than that of succeeding cycles. The Thirty Years War ended in 1648 and the scientific revolution thereafter created increasing prosperity until 1720.

The Bank of England was chartered in 1694 and the Banque Générale de France in 1716. They were the first national fractional banks and so able to create far more credit than had been possible before. The newly available credit enabled stock-market booms in Britain and France. Morgan Stanley Research shows South

Sea Company shares rose 1,000% in 18 months in 1719–20 and fell 84% in the following six months. The Banque Générale de France could issue paper money as well as create credit, so speculation was much more intense in France. Mississippi Company shares rose 6,200% in 13 months and fell 99% in the following 13 months. This disastrous experiment with paper money kept many countries on some form of metallic monetary standard for most of the time up to the First World War. As a result, not only were prices little different in many countries in 1913 than in the early 18th century, but gradual harmonisation of currencies led to significant globalisation from the end of the Napoleonic Wars to the First World War.

The second credit bubble was an urban phenomenon and its collapse wreaked havoc in London society, and even more so in Paris. Attempts to construct wage and price series indicate downward pressure on living standards until Britain lost the American colonies and the French economy descended into the French Revolution. Crashing asset prices stranded a lot of debt, causing widespread bankruptcies and generating a lot of fear. The resulting losses forced banks to call loans from even creditworthy debtors, causing significant debt liquidation that slowed financial activity sharply until banks were recapitalised. Fear of another credit bubble made banks keep lending standards tough for a long time.

Hedge financing soon dominated the financial system, credit eventually stabilised and the third credit cycle began. Asset prices began to rise and firms with the most aggressive financial practices began to accrue a disproportionate share of the profits. Greed and inflation during the Napoleonic Wars (1799–1815) encouraged lenders to drop the need for borrowers to be able to repay principal out of cash flow, causing some borrowers to redefine liquidity from 'a sufficient stock of liquid assets' to 'the ability to borrow more'. Such debtors depended on liquid financial markets to refinance debt as it came due, and inevitably some failed in the periodic liquidity squeezes. However, more prudent entities garnering cheap assets from the failures easily contained the defaults after the Napoleonic Wars ended and after the Bank of England began to redeem notes for gold in 1821.

When defaults were easily contained in liquidity squeezes and asset prices had risen for long enough, financial markets were primed for Ponzi loans, whereby pledged assets became sufficient security for loans. A big expansion in the number of banks and a flood of Mexican silver encouraged US lenders to drop the need for borrowers to be able to pay interest out of cash, radically altering the use of credit. Speculating on rising asset prices became the most profitable use of borrowed money. An ever-rising proportion funded real-estate purchases and the land credit boom began. Rising debt funding real-estate purchases created a credit bubble – a spiral of rising property prices creating a greater demand for real estate, which raised property prices even higher, creating even more demand. For example, the value of real estate in Mobile, Alabama, a gulf coast city, was $1.3 million in 1831 and $27.5 million in 1837.

The money to pay the interest and principal on all the added debt had to come from either the owners' incomes or the sale of the properties, so its viability depended on income and/or real-estate prices rising – the reverse of the self-liquidating debt that had stabilised the credit structure earlier in the cycle. The stock market warned trouble was coming by falling by a third in 1835–36, but the real-estate spiral continued until a peak in the British economy in 1836 shrank its demand for cotton in early 1837. The inflow of Mexican silver dried up at the same time, and the resulting reduction in the flow of credit burst the property bubble and the panic of 1837 ended the third credit cycle.

Debt liquidation and deflation began. From 1837 to 1843, the year stock and wholesale prices and the economy hit a trough, the value of Mobile real estate plummeted to $8.7 million, real investment fell 23% and the money supply shrank 34%. The Federal Bankruptcy Act of 1842 wiped out $450 million of debts and bank assets dropped from $707 million to $393 million, the worst fall in the history of the series. Almost half the nation's banks restructured or closed and eight states and one territory defaulted. The real economy recovered much faster from the depression (regaining trend in 1845) than prices and financial markets. Wholesale prices and stocks did not regain the 1830s highs until 1863.

Deflation is the normal state of a free-market economy not suffering from excessive money growth because increasing productivity lowers prices while wages remain stable. The US grew much faster in the 19th century than in the 20th (albeit from a far lower base) and significant inflation occurred in the war of 1812 and the Civil War. Even so, in 1900 consumer prices were down by about half and wholesale prices were down by about three-eighths from their 1800 levels. The Civil War notwithstanding, the overall US economy was relatively stable and prosperous from 1845 to 1873 when over-expansion in industry and railroads caused a sharp economic and financial contraction. In addition, America demonetised silver in 1873. This temporarily slowed the rise in bank reserves and money supply, so the slowdown was worse in the US than in Europe – although far milder than the

Figure 1 **US total debt-to-GDP ratio**

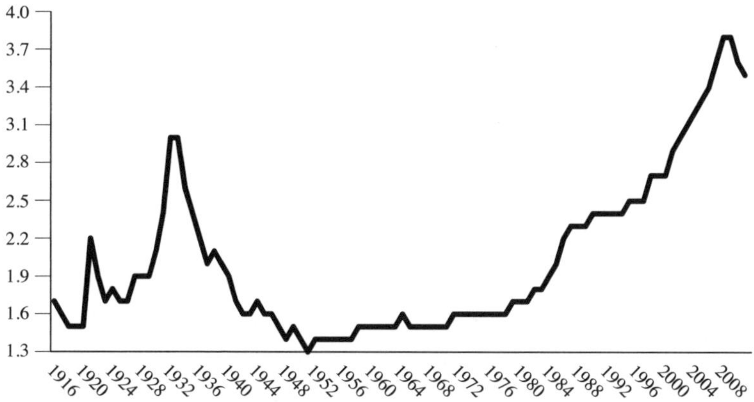

Source: Historical Statistics of the United States from Colonial Times to 1970; Federal Reserve Z1 Releases; Lombard Street Research

1837–43 depression, as bank assets fell only slightly, from $3.2 billion in June 1875 to $3.1 billion in June 1878.

The depression tightened lending standards considerably, initiating a second period of relative stability that ended with the outbreak of war in 1914. Even though every country apart from the US went off the gold standard in 1914 and prices soared, GDP rose faster than debt in the First World War (see Figure 1), so the debt-to-GDP ratio fell until 1921. It then soared because GDP fell sharply. Debt rose faster than GDP during most of the 1920s and, as a result, stock prices soared almost six times from 1921 to 1929. The stock-market crash in 1929 ended the credit cycle and initiated the fourth major debt liquidation. The stock market lost 88% of its value and the money supply fell 31%, while GDP fell 46% and investment fell almost 80%. By contrast, debt fell only 12% and the debt-to-GDP ratio soared to double the 1920

level in 1933. Excessive debt caused massive business failures
and widespread unemployment. The scale of the financial losses
and business failures collapsed the monetary system, the gold
exchange standard, in 1931.

Governments use excessive credit growth and inflation to increase their share of GDP

Government spending under the gold standard was typically in the
mid-single-digit range. All countries on the gold standard, apart
from the US, came off it at the outbreak of the First World War,
causing monetary chaos with a hodgepodge of open, partially
open and closed capital accounts plus fixed, floating and managed
foreign-exchange rates. National monetary policies had created
inflation rates that ranged from excessive to hyper. The UK
insisted it should return to the gold standard at the pre-war parity,
which would have been unbearably deflationary. Furthermore,
European governments and central bankers hated the limits that
the gold standard had placed on them, so they sought a new monetary system that would give them the freedom to create as much
debt as they wanted. The Genoa Conference in 1922 resolved all
these factors into the gold exchange standard, which tried to:

- bring order to the monetary chaos;
- validate past debt growth and inflation;
- enable future debt growth and inflation.

The gold exchange standard failed in the first objective, but
succeeded brilliantly in the second and third – the important ones

to European governments. The dollar remained the only truly convertible currency. Other currencies were not convertible into gold coins, only into large bars reserved for international transactions. Ordinary citizens could not exchange notes and securities for gold. In addition, it enabled the UK to hold bank reserves in dollars as well as gold, and other countries to hold bank reserves in dollars and sterling as well as gold. This system did not restrict British balance of payments deficits and inflation because most other countries did not redeem their pounds for dollars or gold. Instead, they held the sterling as bank reserves and inflated their domestic money supplies accordingly, unleashing a credit-fuelled inflationary boom in the UK and continental Europe.

The UK induced the US to accumulate sterling debt to minimise the UK's loss of dollars and gold. Rising sterling reserves reduced the US share of global gold reserves from 1923 to 1930, even though US prices remained stable in contrast to European inflation. France followed an anti-inflationary policy too, but demanded gold to settle outstanding balances, so its share of global gold reserves more than doubled from 8.2% in 1923 to 19.2% in 1930. By contrast, the British share fell by almost a quarter from 8.6% to 6.6% while sterling liabilities soared. As a result, foreign exchange, most of it sterling, constituted 35% of European central bank reserves in 1930. This growth in reserves enabled a credit bubble in Europe and the US.

In 1931, France tried to convert its sterling reserves into gold. The UK could not comply and went off the gold exchange standard, which collapsed the credit bubble and the international payments system simultaneously. Foreign exchange fell to 8% of European central bank reserves in 1932, which shrank bank balance sheets, credit and money supplies by unprecedented amounts. As a result, defaults soared, causing a panic that induced runs on banks and turned the severe recession (due to the earlier stock-market crashes and Smoot Hawley tariffs) into the Great Depression.

The gold exchange standard was a badly flawed system, so this dismal ending was inevitable. Capital accounts were open, exchange rates fixed and interest rates under national control. This contravened the what should be by now well-known principle that no country can maintain a fixed exchange rate, an open capital account and an independent monetary policy simultaneously (the 'impossible trinity'). As a result, the big imbalances in credit, trade and gold holdings grew until the system collapsed.

The gold exchange standard overvalued sterling relative to gold and the dollar. Gresham's Law says that 'bad money drives out good if their exchange rate is set by law', so sterling replaced the dollar in international transactions. As a result, the US and France together held 57.9% of global gold reserves in 1930. Public convertibility had prevented lopsided distributions of gold under the classic gold standard, but the gold exchange standard eliminated this crucial adjustment mechanism. Its lack was immaterial as long as foreign exchange was 'as good as gold', but disastrous when it was not.

National control of interest rates creates big differences in inflation rates. Floating exchange rates can neutralise inflation rate differentials or capital controls can insulate nations from global capital flows. Neither was available under the gold exchange standard, so sterling liabilities accumulated until the system imploded, turning a severe recession into the Great Depression. President Hoover began the socialist policies that made President Roosevelt famous, yet US real GNP fell 31% in the 1930s compared with 8% in the UK, which did not intervene. Governments, central bankers, economists and academics blame the gold standard for the Great Depression – despite this contrary empirical evidence. It was not the gold standard but the deliberate perversion of it into the gold exchange standard to perpetuate inflation that caused the Great Depression. Nevertheless, the 'official' version has prevailed.

The next monetary system, instituted by the Bretton Woods Agreement in 1944, turned over complete control of money supplies to governments and central banks – i.e. mandated universal fiat money. The agreement was promoted as an intermediate step towards a return to the gold standard. The dollar would be a reserve currency until global trade could reallocate gold from the severe misdistribution resulting from the gold exchange standard. However, John Maynard Keynes, a principal architect, had a very different vision. Massive government intervention would reduce unemployment and keep it low. Furthermore, the agreement established the International Monetary Fund (IMF) and the International Bank for Reconstruction and Development (IBRD), which later merged to become the World Bank, to aid this government intervention.

The IMF was to oversee adherence to the fixed exchange rates, permitting adjustments when necessary, and to lend to countries with trade deficits so they could continue trading until the deficits were corrected. The IBRD was to enable a speedy post-war recovery by lending its own funds, underwriting private loans and issuing securities to raise new funds for economic development. The IBRD was meant to wither away after about five years (as Lenin claimed communist governments would), but a major problem arose almost immediately.

The IMF's modest credit facilities could not cope with Western Europe's huge balance of payments deficits. The US was running huge balance of trade surpluses, so its foreign-exchange reserves were immense and growing. Overcoming the consequent shortage of dollars required this flow be reversed. The US created the required balance of payments deficits by setting up the Marshall Plan in 1947 to provide the large-scale aid needed to rebuild Europe.

Fixed exchange rates expressed in gold were the only part of the classic gold standard retained in the new system. The need for the Marshall Plan ended any pretence of markets reallocating gold reserves and enabling a return to the classic gold standard. By contrast, the lesson of the impossible trinity had been learned. Governments considered unemployment to be the most pressing problem and most countries had placed restrictions on capital flows, enabling the fixed exchange-rate regime to accommodate the low interest rates deemed necessary to reduce unemployment.

The Bretton Woods period has been called the golden age of capitalism because of the high growth rates in Europe and North America. However, the depression and the Second World War had created two decades of pent-up consumer demand while post-war reconstruction and an unparalleled baby boom ensured strong growth would continue for a long time. Moreover, very high private savings and the very liquid financial system enabled high levels of investment. Only the availability of raw materials and labour restrained economic growth.

It is debatable whether Bretton Woods hindered or helped the strong underlying economic forces, but two unforeseen events consigned it to the dustbin of history. First, the Eurodollar market began to undermine the effectiveness of capital controls in the

1960s, at the same time as high levels of employment began to reduce the desire to maintain low interest rates and the capital controls to accommodate them. Second, and much more important, price stability depended on US policy.

US inflation soared from under 2% in 1965 to over 6% in 1970 as a result of President Johnson's 'guns and butter' policy. Fixed exchange rates transmitted the US inflation, at least in part, to all countries in the regime and price stability became the paramount concern. Milton Friedman had long argued that the best way to avoid foreign inflationary pressures is a flexible exchange-rate regime. He won the argument when President Nixon closed the gold window on 15 August 1971, ending both the Bretton Woods Agreement and any connection between the global monetary system and the mistakenly maligned gold standard.

Soon after the gold window closed, major countries began to let their exchange rates float to avoid importing inflation. In addition, international focus on increasing trade encouraged the opening of capital accounts which are equal and opposite to current accounts. The theory was that capital liberalisation would not only increase global trade and growth by lowering the cost of capital in capital-poor countries and raising the return on capital in capital-rich ones (thereby increasing capital investment and productivity), but also lead to better fiscal and monetary policies. As a result, most major countries had begun to liberalise their capital accounts and allow their exchange rates to float by the early 1980s, ushering in a new era of globalisation that was in many ways comparable to the pre-First World War globalisation under the classic gold standard.

Demobilising from the Second World War and the return to hedge financing (because of the fear generated by the losses suffered in the Great Depression) produced falling debt-to-GDP ratios until 1951. GDP grew quickly in the 1950s and 1960s, but rising speculative debt drove debt-to-GDP ratios up. Predictably, default rates rose, even though soaring inflation during the 1970s bailed out financial institutions that would otherwise have failed. The Volcker credit crunch in the early 1980s reversed inflation, which extended the rising defaults into non-financial business. Despite this, debt-to-GDP ratios continued to soar because falling inflation encouraged speculation on rising asset prices. The proportion of Ponzi debt rose rapidly, borrowing and lending became totally irrational and the US debt-to-GDP ratio soared to more than a quarter more than the previous all-time high in 1933 (see Figure 1).

Serpents lurk in modern globalisation

The classic gold standard mandated open capital accounts. Many countries did not adopt the gold standard, but its automatic stabilisers had prevented the creation of imbalances in those that did. By contrast, fiat money has no automatic stabilisers. Global capital flows seeking the highest interest rates are big enough to force small countries into monetary easing in booms to discourage capital inflows, and monetary tightening in recessions to discourage capital outflows. This forcing of pro-cyclical monetary policy accentuates the normal cyclical fluctuations. As a result, many small countries have begun either to impose some capital controls or to use a major currency or a currency board to prevent unwanted capital inflows and the resulting outflows from disrupting their economies.

A far worse problem from a global perspective is that countries maintaining open capital accounts have no effective defence from other countries manipulating the exchange rates of their currencies and/or using closed capital accounts and other domestic policies to gain ever-bigger shares of global export markets. Such countries ultimately amass huge current-account surpluses – the Eurasian savings glut. The current account is equal to national saving (government deficits are negative national saving) less domestic investment. National saving was far greater than domestic investment in China, Japan and Germany and far less than domestic investment in the US, the UK and most countries on the north shore of the Mediterranean. Obviously, the net global trade surplus is zero, so the current-account deficits in low-saving countries must offset the surpluses in high-saving ones.

The savers fund the borrowers' deficits, building up huge global imbalances of saving and investment. Real interest rates have trended down from the start of globalisation in the early 1980s. Falling real interest rates prove that the desire to save in the save-and-export countries exceeded the desire to borrow in the borrow-and-spend ones – i.e. the growing surpluses caused the growing deficits. Savers can accumulate surpluses in perpetuity, but the borrowers exhausted their ability to borrow and spend in 2007, causing the Great Recession that began the essential unwinding of the accumulated imbalances in saving and investment. The private sectors in the major deficit countries saved more and spent less, so domestic saving should have replaced foreign saving and current-account deficits should have fallen. This did not happen for two interrelated reasons.

First, fiscal deficits in current-account deficit countries soared, mopping up the rise in private savings. Second, surplus countries continued their mercantilist policies, even though their surpluses sent good money after bad in some cases. The only way to reduce the massive imbalance of saving and investment that the Eurasian savings glut has amassed is for the surplus countries to spend more and the deficit ones to save more. Slowing growth has put the onus on the surplus countries to spend more because (as Chapter 4 explains) the only way deficit countries as a whole can save more would be to export more to and/or import less from surplus countries. China has co-operated and its current-account surplus is close to zero, but northern Europe is doing everything it can to force the peripheral euro-zone states to save more without spending more itself. This policy is bankrupting the peripheral states and, if continued long enough, will bankrupt the core states too.

The fifth major credit bubble has ended

The theory underlying today's financial system is that all risk can be hedged and the difference between the return on a security and the cost of hedging its risk can be skimmed risk-free. This vision of risk-free return encouraged ever-increasing leverage and debt-to-GDP ratios soared. However, all transactions have counterparties and rising leverage raised the probability of counterparties failing to fulfil their obligations. The ever-increasing leverage created a string of five crises caused by counterparty default:

- the Latin American credit bubble that burst in the early 1980s;
- the savings and loan debt bubble that burst in the early 1990s;
- the Asian debt bubble that burst in 1997;

- the Long-Term Capital Management (LTCM)/Russian credit bubble that burst in 1998;
- the housing bubble that burst with the subprime mortgage crisis in 2007–08.

The first four crises were localised and their bursting was easily contained. None of them created major problems, but the occurrence of so many crises in such a short time was a warning sign that the fifth major credit bubble was approaching its end. No one heeded the warnings and most banks kept increasing their leverage, up to 50 times net tangible equity and more. Furthermore, nearly all bank balance sheets contain hidden losses because loans to weak borrowers and the securities of distressed governments remain valued at cost until the borrower defaults. These unrealised losses make many banks technically insolvent, so most cannot afford to book losses – even if writing down debts would benefit both the lender and the borrower. They would have minimal or negative net tangible equity if they had to mark their assets to market, so any default could be catastrophic. They must use most, if not all, of their resources to keep their weak borrowers afloat.

As a result, the US was only one of many countries in which credit grew at alarming rates until their private sectors ran out of the ability to borrow. However, the post-credit-bubble collapse sequence of events has been far less severe than in previous cycles. The unlimited credit of fiat money allowed:

- central banks to provide commercial banks with far more reserves than they could use;
- government spending and fiscal deficits to soar;

- governments to guarantee bank liabilities and move bad private debt onto public balance sheets simultaneously in a desperate effort to avoid the deflationary effects of credit liquidation.

These initiatives have prevented money supplies from falling at the high rates of previous cycles – so far. This outcome resembles Japan's two lost decades since its debt-fuelled and multi-faceted asset bubble collapsed in 1990. Japanese government debt soared past non-financial private debt outstanding (which has been trending down) and total debt has risen to about 500% of GDP. Even though Japanese interest rates are ludicrously low, the immense burden of this debt has held the Japanese economy stagnant.

Several developed countries are likely to follow this general pattern in the next few years. Total UK debt is at about the same level as Japan's, and other developed countries' debts are rising rapidly. The BIS and others estimate that debt above about 90% of GDP for households and non-financial corporations and above about 85% of GDP for governments slows growth. The BIS studied 18 countries in 2010. No country had all three ratios below the benchmarks and three, the UK, Canada and Portugal, had all three ratios above the benchmarks. The median was above the benchmarks in two categories then and would now be far above in the third, government debt.

Overwhelming levels of debt and chronic current-account imbalances are limiting global growth, and both must be reduced before normal growth can resume. Progress toward their resolution has been and will continue to be slow until the looming European sovereign debt/banking crisis initiates the deflation that will hasten it. The next chapter explains the six signs that will indicate progress towards the goal of optimum growth.

2

The six signs of progress

In the past, rapidly rising demand and inflation as a result of major wars, such as the First World War, created credit bubbles. Sharp drops in demand and inflation at the ends of the wars burst the bubbles, causing a tidal wave of defaults and depression, as in 1920–21. During that depression, the Treasury balanced the budget and the Federal Reserve raised interest rates. These policies ended war-induced speculation while defaults wrote off bad debts. A 'double indemnity' clause required bank shareholders to invest an amount equal to the par value of their holdings if necessary, ensuring that banks operated with safety cushions and could absorb the losses. Nominal GNP plunged in 1921, but businesses saw opportunities and banks were willing and able to lend.

Tax cuts increased private demand and US federal debt falling from $25.6 billion to $16.5 billion from 1919 to 1929 enabled strong private investment to create the roaring 20s. Unfortunately, those days and those policies are long gone. That was the last non-inflationary boom. Governments ignored the dotcom bust in 2000 and markets corrected the imbalances with a minor recession. The short duration of the depression in the 1920s and the minor recession in 2000–01 show that markets can correct economic and financial imbalances quickly and efficiently.

By contrast, government intervention caused the so-called Great Depression in the US in the 1930s. Other countries had far smaller depressions – even the European countries that created the inflationary credit-fuelled boom that ultimately collapsed the monetary system in 1931 (see Chapter 4) – because the laissez-faire policies of the 1920–21 depression produced the same shallow depression in the 1930s. Similarly, government interference produced weak and inflationary growth in the credit-fuelled 2002–07 recovery that collapsed into the Great Recession in 2007–09. Government interference is not required; it is counterproductive.

The 1920–21 depression was short because financial markets:

- cut off the accumulation of bad debts;
- wrote off all the bad debt;
- recapitalised banks where required.

These have always been immediate priorities to restore growth after credit bubble collapses.

Nominal GDP normally falls faster than debt outstanding during implementation of these priorities. Avoiding this short period of intense pain is impossible. Sustainable growth cannot start until business is willing and able to borrow and banks are willing and able to lend, which requires the completion of all three priorities. Japan and Ireland have made structural changes and undergone significant deflation, but neither has restored optimal growth because neither has fully implemented the three priorities. Japan has not written off all the bad debt and Ireland has not recapitalised its banks. Their continuing plight shows that adding debt before the three priorities are completed is

counterproductive. Most of it will end up being written off, mul-
tiplying the total amount of losses. Most developed countries are
making this mistake.

The consensus cure-all since the Penn Central Transportation
Company bailout (see Chapter 9) creates artificially low interest
rates and huge fiscal deficits, bringing future saving and investment, i.e. future growth, back to the present. Continual borrowing
from the future has weakened balance sheets and reduced creditworthiness until, as always, the credit bubble collapsed because
incomes could no longer pay the interest on the debt outstanding.
Credit bubbles are discussed in Chapter 3. Here it suffices to say
that government attempts to avoid the deflation that always followed credit bubble collapses in the past are creating so much
new debt that one country has already defaulted and several more
will. More debt can never solve the problem of inability to service
the debt already outstanding.

Furthermore, creating a sustainable recovery requires the
average interest rate to be lower than the nominal growth rate
– otherwise rising interest rates can raise debt-to-GDP ratios –
even if debt already outstanding falls. Zero interest rate policies
and short-term borrowing in many developed countries have
minimised interest rates, yet nominal growth remains lower in
most because they suffer from falling or negative population
growth, rising dependency ratios, falling productivity growth,
falling inflation and the as yet unacknowledged need for structural reform in government and labour.

Fiat money removing credit limits has enabled developed
country government spending typically to quintuple from about
10% of GDP in the 1920s to about 50% in 2013. Governments
ran out of ways to increase the proportion of GDP they could

raise in taxes years ago. Since then they have borrowed ever-increasing amounts to enable them to spend a rising share of GDP. As a result, some have run out of borrowing power and now must delever simultaneously with the private sector. Improving their trade balances is the only way they can accomplish this goal. Few will succeed because their labour generally cannot compete with that of emerging countries. Normally, countries regain competitiveness by devaluing their currencies, but mercantilist currency manipulation and membership in the euro are preventing those that need to devalue most from doing so. As a result, only structural reform and deflation can restore sustainable growth in developed countries today.

Deflation is the natural outcome of deleverage. Both repayment and default reduce money supplies by the principal amount of debt liquidated. Default is more painful because it also reduces equity capital by the principal amount less the amount recovered. Banks are highly levered, so particularly hurt by defaults. Some banks have assets 50 times their capital, which means a 2% loss on their assets would wipe out their capital, making them insolvent. Their consequent recapitalisations would reduce the money supply further, unless the funds came from foreign investment. Central banks are monetising government debt (read printing money) to offset these downward pressures on money supplies.

Financial markets want governments to print money because it nurtures hopes that the resulting inflation will raise incomes and asset prices enough to service the outstanding debts. Unfortunately, current conditions are uniquely bad. The collapse of the biggest credit bubble in history makes this the first time that the developed world's public sector, banking system and households have all become insolvent at the same time. Usually two of the three have been able to rescue the third. The Great Depression of the 1930s was the worst ever because only governments had access to credit after the monetary system collapsed in 1931. Today many developed-country governments are insolvent and the others are rapidly becoming so. Printing money cannot alleviate such widespread solvency problems. Only develerage and restructuring can do this, and neither has progressed more than imperceptibly in the five years since the credit structure began to crumble. As a result, none of the six indicators of emergence from the problems caused by the credit bubble collapse have appeared.

We will know success when we see ...

1 The financial sector has stabilised and lending is rising

Sustainable output growth requires money growth, which, in turn, depends on borrowers that are both creditworthy and willing to borrow and banks that are both willing and able to lend. A lack of willing borrowers collapsed the credit bubble in 2007–08. This caused a sharp drop in asset prices and a rise in defaulted loans, which greatly reduced the number of both creditworthy and willing borrowers. Worse, the defaults decimated the capital of banks, so the number of banks willing and able to lend plummeted and credit conditions tightened commensurately. Even so, soaring fiscal deficits and central banks printing money kept both output growth and money supplies stable to rising in many countries – but at the expense of rapidly rising public debt-to-GDP ratios.

Some countries have already run out of borrowing power. Others are following close behind. Recapitalising banks is the most urgent priority to stabilise the financial sector, particularly in Europe. However, governments that have run out of borrowing power have no resources to initiate bank recapitalisation and their economies could collapse without significant outside assistance. Few developed countries have stable financial sectors, and the longer those that do not have stable financial sectors delay this essential first step, the greater the danger of their economies collapsing.

2 Structural reforms have unleashed non-bank private-sector growth

After a credit bubble collapse, significant private deleverage is required before sustainable growth can occur. This causes contractions in the money supply and output, while recapitalising banks (as required in point 1) deflates the money supply and output further. Deflation reveals the need to reduce the excessive costs that arose in the credit bubble – government, financial services and labour in the current cycle. The creation of central banks and income tax in the early 20th century ushered in the era of big government.

Government spending has risen from 10% or less of GNP in the 1920s (US federal tax revenues peaked at 7½% of GNP in 1921) to 35–55% in 2012. Few countries can prosper with non-productive governments spending half the national output. Governments must reduce the share of GDP they spend permanently by focusing on and reducing the costs of activities they can carry out more efficiently than the private sector, such as providing the social safety net voters want. Anything else is unaffordable. They must also remove impediments to non-bank private-sector growth. Then, and only then, can the monstrous government deficits and debts be reduced.

3 Credible medium-term plans to reduce fiscal deficits are in place

US and Canadian federal governments passed budgets in 1971, and every year thereafter, that predicted their deficits (originally incurred to stimulate recovery from the 1970 recession) would be eliminated in the third year after that budget. Those deficits did not end until 1995. Few budget projections are credible because governments normally forecast higher-than-trend nominal growth, add a fiscal multiplier to the optimistic growth assumption and disregard the normal behaviour modification to mitigate the effect of tax increases, so revenues usually fall short of projections.

Governments also project spending growth far below GDP growth – even though spending growth usually exceeds GDP growth by a wide margin. Furthermore, the same governments that trumpet the virtues of fiscal stimulation neglect the fact that fiscal restraint subtracts from GDP growth. The longer the forecast, the further revenue and expenditure projections stray from reality, so medium-term budget forecasts are usually rubbish. Hard times increase scepticism, so making credible forecasts of deficit reduction will become ever more difficult.

4 Exports are growing significantly faster than imports

Investment drives capitalist economies by creating demand that did not exist before. However, the ample spare capacity in post-credit-bubble-crash economies needs little investment, so rising net exports are usually required to stimulate the investment needed to kick-start sustainable recovery. Currency devaluation improves the trade balances of countries with low to negative inflation, but the inability of euro-zone states to devalue is blocking their efforts to recover from the collapse of the credit bubble.

Outside the euro zone, competitive devaluation is impeding not only global recovery, but also the deleverage necessary to correct international imbalances of saving and investment.

5 Rising private investment is driving growth

Investment often exceeds domestic saving in the recovery from collapsed credit bubbles. The trade and current-account balances then must turn from positive to negative to import the saving needed to fund the investment. Current-account deficits are normal when investment is driving growth.

6 The housing market has stabilised

Household net worth usually greatly exceeds business net worth, government net worth and the sum of business and government net worth. Household balance sheets are the foundation of the credit structure. Housing is by far the biggest asset most people own, so their equity in their homes is the biggest single part of the stock of national saving. Falling house prices erode the stock of saving supporting the credit structure and ultimately cause banking crises. House prices must be at least stable to anchor the credit structure. The housing industry also has a big multiplier effect, as every new unit requires appliances, furniture, furnishings and transport. It is important to note that the housing market cannot be considered stable until interest rates have returned to more normal levels. UK house prices look especially vulnerable to future rising interest rates unless deleveraging accelerates.

This chapter has shown that markets correct the imbalances of booms with much less disruption without than with government intervention. It has also shown that the removal of credit limits enabled governments to quintuple their share of GDP, but they are reaching the limits of their expansion. A period of deleverage and reconstruction is required, and the appearance of the six signs cited in this chapter will show when the required adjustments have been completed and the next expansion can begin. The following chapters explain why current financial conditions are unique, starting with an examination of the seven tailwinds that eased emergence from past crises but have now become headwinds.

3

This time it really is different

Deferred consumption (read saving) is the source of the investment that creates the means of production and productivity. Capitalism cannot function without saving and investment, so the postponement of consumption is the basic element of wealth creation. People need the prospect of more consumption than would otherwise be possible at a future date to defer present consumption. Interest provides the surest way to increase savings to the amount needed for the prospective future consumption, so interest is the cost borrowers must pay to induce others to defer the consumption needed to fund their desire to invest. The natural interest rate is the most risk-free rate that, in the absence of external interference and with reasonable increments for the various forms of risk (credit, liquidity and market), will equate the desire to save with the desire to invest.

The natural rate of interest is neither observable nor static. It varies as desires to save and to invest change. The market interest rate below the natural rate makes investment more profitable than usual, raising the desire to invest and reducing the desire to save. Investment will increase and saving will fall until the market rate rises to the natural rate. The market rate above the natural rate will make investment less profitable than usual, reducing the desire to invest and raising the desire to save. Investment will fall and saving will rise until the market rate falls to the natural rate.

The financial system's function is to collect savings and distribute them to those who can best use them. Market interest rates fluctuating above and below natural interest rates distributed savings well in the classic gold standard because neither governments nor central banks manipulated interest rates. The automatic stabilisers embodied in the classic gold standard kept market interest rates near their natural rates for over seven decades by mandating that gold and currency be interchangeable at a fixed and constant rate and bank reserves be held in gold. Bank reserve ratios were also fixed, so a given flow of gold into banks from private hands or international transactions would raise bank reserves and the money supply by a known amount. Similarly, a given outflow of gold would lower bank reserves and the money supply by a known amount.

Currency convertibility and the need to settle international balances in gold meant that countries with current-account deficits in excess of capital inflows automatically experienced deflationary gold outflows. The loss of gold triggered a rise in short-term interest rates and a fall in prices until the outflow stopped. This not only made the chronic current-account deficits and surpluses that have plagued countries since the classic gold standard ended at the outbreak of the First World War impossible, but also prevented governments from pursuing inflationary policies. The rising short-term rates raised the opportunity cost of holding gold, so bank reserves rose as investors converted gold into interest-bearing paper. Similarly, a gold inflow raised bank reserves, triggering a drop in interest rates and a rise in prices. Falling short-term rates reduced the opportunity cost of holding gold and bank reserves fell as investors converted interest-bearing paper into gold until the inflow was sterilised and interest rates stopped falling.

Gold flows automatically altered short-term interest rates, so they changed frequently. The Bank of England changed the bank rate as many as 24 times in a year, although the odd year passed by with no change. Small interest-rate changes would often stem gold flows, even reverse them. However, reserves were small and flows had to be stopped quickly, so sometimes big changes were needed. The close association between bank reserves and short-term rates stabilised not just output and prices in each country on the gold standard, but financial markets too.

As a result, global trade in the 19th century was bigger relative to GDP than it is today, inflation was non-existent, output grew faster and interest rates were more stable and more uniform across national boundaries. Chapter 1 showed that governments have taken every opportunity in the past nine decades to break the limitations the classic gold standard had placed on them. The result has been Wall Street crashes, a monetary system collapse, the Great Depression, the worst inflation since the fall of Rome, chronic current-account surpluses and deficits, and the rise and bursting of the biggest credit bubble in history. In contrast to their supposed independence, the only thing that has prevented political manipulation of central banks is a combination of exceptionally strong heads, such as William McChesney Martin, Paul Volcker and John Crow, operating in a high-inflation environment. In a low or falling inflation environment, central bank heads that act independently get fired (James Coyne) or are not reappointed regardless of superior performance (Paul Volcker).

By contrast, Arthur Burns, a former Fed chairman, described

central bank parameters well when he said that the Fed must act as the president wishes or it would lose its independence. Continuous political pressure forced central banks to keep market interest rates below the natural rate to stimulate growth for most of the past 90 years. The huge current-account surpluses generated by China, Japan, the oil-producing countries and northern Europe, especially since the turn of the century, flooded the rest of the world with saving, adding to the downward pressure on interest rates. Interest rates are the time cost of money. Current interest rates give money negative to minimal time cost. The extra investment and consumption enabled by the ridiculously low interest rates has merely borrowed from future investment and consumption, while the added debt has reduced the borrowers' creditworthiness.

Since the future is inherently uncertain, the borrowed-from-the-future investments were even more speculative than those from saving, so the debt added by the artificially low interest rates was speculative and Ponzi debt (see Chapter 1). The only way to maintain the long-term stability the classic gold standard achieved would be to raise interest rates enough above the natural rate to reverse the borrowing from the future and quash speculation, but politics prevents that. As a result, fiscal and monetary policies have riddled public and private balance sheets with so much bad debt that the US, Japan, the UK and Europe are all in liquidity traps.

Liquidity traps occur when short-term interest rates are near zero and raising the monetary base does not cause money growth and rising prices, i.e. when overlevered borrowers and lenders have neutered monetary policy. Fiscal policy then is responsible for stimulation, but the fiscal deficits in the countries in liquidity traps are already unsustainable, so the looming European sovereign debt/banking crisis described in later chapters will flip four decades of borrowing from the future into a payback era. The last flip into a payback era occurred when the collapse of the Credit Anstalt Bank in 1931 caused a domino effect of defaults that collapsed the credit bubble that the gold exchange standard created. A European crisis could cause a similar domino effect of defaults.

As in the 1930s, this flip would correct the massive international imbalances of saving and investment and erase the existing mountain of bad debt, thereby creating the conditions for a return to sustainable growth. The corrections would have to include a major restructuring of government and financial markets to avoid a return to past bad habits and a similar crisis recurring in the future. Developed countries' governments quintupled their share of GDP in the past 90 years. They produce little and now spend about half their national GDP doing it. Few countries can prosper with half their GDP going into non-productive uses and efforts to downsize governments have begun, albeit unsuccessfully so far. They should become more successful as downsizing progresses because governments have grown most and have the least to show for it. The corrections should also reduce financial markets to their proper function of intermediating saving. The 2008 banking crisis created a widespread call for bank reform, but the unbelievably big, wealthy and powerful bank lobby has derailed or watered down every potentially meaningful reform. The eurozone sovereign debt crisis is providing a second opportunity.

Solvent governments have often rescued the private sector from the banking crises resulting from burst credit bubbles, as Sweden and Finland did in the 1990s. Solvent and liquid private sectors have often rescued governments from intolerable debt burdens, usually after wars. The successes mentioned above have created the belief that countries can always inflate and/or grow their way out of excessive deficits and debts, and few can see any reason why proper policies cannot enable governments, especially in the euro zone, to do that now. They cannot because the situation is unique. Both the private sector and the public sector are overly indebted.

Usually, household balance sheets can fund the long-term borrowing needs of government and business, but households are over-indebted and must pay down debt. Normally, banks can fund the short-term needs of households and business, but banks in many countries are both over-indebted and undercapitalised, so have to shrink their balance sheets. The massive borrowing power of governments is normally enough to fund the recapitalisation of banks when they run into trouble, but most developed country governments are under pressure to reduce their borrowing needs. Ireland and the UK's experience with nationalising banks has shown the pressure this puts on public-sector finances – no wonder core states such as France and Germany are reluctant to tackle their woefully undercapitalised banking sectors.

Supranational agencies, such as the International Monetary Fund, are the lenders of last resort, but their borrowing power depends on the credit of the constituent nations, which is diminishing almost daily. In short, for the first time in history, there is no strong balance sheet to fund the recovery of the entities in trouble. Non-financial corporations, especially in the US, have the strongest balance sheets. They are not big enough to create a recovery, but are big enough to lead it if, as and when conditions become favourable.

In addition to the absence of a balance sheet to fund recovery, the following seven factors that helped both developed and emerging countries to grow and/or inflate their way out of severe debt and deficit problems in the past have reversed:

- **Positive demographics** expanded the labour supply and created demand, making growth the default economic setting.
- **Loose monetary policy** kept private-sector borrowing costs down, encouraging inflation and investment.
- **Technological advancements** created productivity gains.
- **Devaluation** lowered export prices and raised import prices, enabling additional growth through net trade.
- **Export demand** was created by rapid growth in the rest of the world.
- **End to war-related spending** gave governments ample scope for the spending and tax cuts needed to stimulate growth.
- **Healthy private-sector balance sheets** allowed the private sector to take up the slack as the government retrenched or healthy government balance sheets funded the restructuring and recapitalisation of banks.

Headwinds

All of those tailwinds in preceding cycles have become headwinds to a greater or lesser degree for all developed countries in this cycle. However, they all greatly affect euro-zone states, so the following discussion concentrates on them and brings in other countries only when they are greatly affected. The headwinds are:

- negative demographics;

- rising costs of entitlements;
- monetary policy impotence;
- no devaluation safety valve;
- increasing global competition;
- austerity;
- no healthy balance sheet.

Negative demographics

Figure 2 shows the medium variant of the UN's 2010 estimates of the population growth of the five largest European economies and the US. Growth is falling or negative in them all, so populations are ageing. This is the long-predicted demographic time bomb, which is causing rapidly increasing age-related spending at the same time as labour force growth rates are shrinking to

Figure 2   Estimated annual population growth rates
%

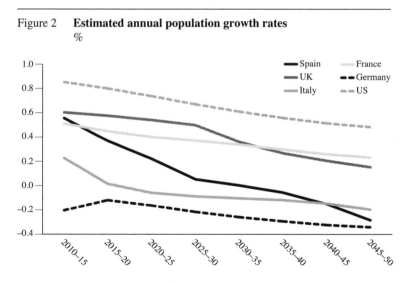

Sources: World Population Prospects: The 2010 Revision; Lombard Street Research

negative. Labour force and income growth in developed countries has become too small to pay for the rising costs of the entitlements, particularly age-related, that governments have promised in perpetuity.

Rising costs of entitlements

The costs of expected entitlements exceeding the willingness of work forces to pay for them are the main cause of the widespread deficit financing in developed countries. The next chapter will look at government policy errors in detail. Here it suffices to say that it had been known for decades before the credit bubble collapsed in 2007–08 that age-related spending would accelerate precisely when the growth rates of labour forces were slowing and turning negative. However, governments never realistically assessed the sustainability of their programmes. Instead, they used overly optimistic forecasts to justify minimal changes that could, at best, only postpone crises for a few years. As a result, sovereign debt-to-GDP ratios soared to the extent that some governments can no longer borrow in financial markets at reasonable rates. Clearly, most developed country governments cannot sustain their programmes – even in this period of ultra-low interest rates – in perpetuity without radical changes.

Ageing populations are causing increased spending and impeding growth. The Bank for International Settlements (BIS) working paper no. 300, *The Future of Public Debt: Prospects and Implications*, published in March 2010, showed that the debt-to-GDP ratios of all 12 countries studied – Austria, France, Germany, Greece, Ireland, Italy, Japan, Netherlands, Portugal, Spain, the UK and the US – would spiral out of control if:

- government revenue and non-age-related spending remained a constant percentage of GDP;
- Congressional Budget Office and European Commission projections for age-related spending proved correct.

Reducing structural deficits by 1% of GDP a year for five years would still leave all the countries with soaring debt-to-GDP ratios for the 30 years projected – except Italy, where debt would stabilise at about 100% of GDP. If, in addition, age-related spending were frozen at the estimated 2011 level of GDP, only Austria, Germany and Netherlands would have peak debt-to-GDP ratios under 100%. Japan and the UK would be worst off with sovereign debts over 300% of GDP, with the US not far behind at about 230%, including state and local debt. The rest would have debt-to-GDP ratios between 100% and 200%.

Sovereign finances have deteriorated since that study. Growth ranging from weak to negative and rising age-related spending have already pushed many sovereign debt-to-GDP ratios past 90% – the point at which both Carmen Reinhart and Kenneth Rogoff and the BIS have shown debt becomes a drag on growth. In addition, most of the euro-zone peripheral states are already in long and deep recessions that are spreading into the core. Contingent liabilities, namely insolvent banking sectors and highly indebted domestic companies, make the problem worse. Most governments have little chance of reversing their rising debt-to-GDP ratios until they restructure their entitlement programmes – and some face other headwinds.

Monetary policy impotence
Chapter 2 showed how the impossible trinity (open capital

accounts, fixed exchange rates and independent monetary policy cannot persist together) ended the gold exchange standard. In theory, the euro conforms to the impossible trinity. Every country in the euro has a fixed exchange rate and an open capital account, and the European Central Bank (ECB) administers a single monetary policy. In practice, however, that single policy has produced a variety of real interest rates. The core consisted of slow-growing and low-inflation states with strong currencies and low nominal interest rates. The periphery consisted of fast-growing and high-inflation countries with weak currencies and high nominal interest rates.

Higher inflation in the peripheral states and low centrally set nominal interest rates created excessively low real interest rates and borrowing soared. This could have been a passport to prosperity, had they used the loans to increase productivity, output and exports. Instead, they wasted the funds on real-estate speculation and increased government largesse – as the US wasted cheap dollar funding on subprime mortgages. Their inflation rates remained higher than those in the core, they became ever more uncompetitive, even within the euro, and their current-account deficits rose. The credit bubble burst and suddenly financial markets demanded ever-rising interest rates to fund their fiscal deficits of up to 10% of GDP and more in the face of rising interest rates.

The difference in national real interest rates was far less than in nominal rates before the euro. People who should have known better hoped that ECB acceptance of all euro-zone sovereign debt as collateral effectively guaranteed repayment, so the credit risk of the various countries' debts was about the same because they would profit greatly if they were. As a result, markets pushed the nominal interest rates in peripheral states down close to those in the core, causing a big difference in real rates, ever-increasing uncompetitiveness and ever-rising current-account deficits until some became unable to pay the interest on their soaring indebtedness.

Now the bubble has burst, deflation in the periphery means real interest rates are too high for these countries and real GDP growth is falling. Central banks are trying to do all they can to raise output and money growth.[2] However, holding interest rates down is financial repression, which transfers funds from savers to the biggest borrowers, i.e. governments, which, in turn curtails investment, productivity and output growth. Furthermore, expanding central bank balance sheets fund asset purchases, so the money growth they create is quickly lost in higher asset prices.

This is postponing not only a collapse in asset prices and consequent deflationary spiral, but also the necessary write-off of bad debts and economic rebalancing. For example, the low interest rates in the UK account for the failure of households to pay off excess mortgage debt. As a result, central banks can create only low-powered money and private-sector debt deflation is frustrating the record-breaking monetary stimulation in developed countries, which, much as they would like to, can neither grow nor inflate their way out of their debt and deficit problems.

No devaluation safety valve

Net export growth is absolutely necessary to raise GDP growth in uncompetitive countries. Currency devaluation increases exports by lowering their prices to foreign buyers and raises the prices of imports to domestic buyers, encouraging the substitution of domestically produced goods for imports. As a result, devaluation is critical to permit a country to grow and/or inflate out of severe debt and deficit problems. An open economy such as Ireland could have returned to prosperity if it had been able to devalue, but it is suffering recession and deflation instead. Differential real interest rates have ultimately caused big enough current-account imbalances in all currency unions (that were not also political unions) to break up the union.

The euro is no exception. Chronic and rising current-account deficits in peripheral states raised their debt burdens far beyond sustainable levels. They must lower their prices to foreign buyers to regain competitiveness, without being able to devalue. This means they must deflate their nominal wages and prices by the amount their currencies would have fallen if they could have devalued. The so-called bailouts, even defaulting on their debts, do not alleviate the need to slash wages and prices because they do not reduce the basic problem: uncompetitiveness causing chronic current-account deficits.

After two bailout packages and defaulting on its privately held debt, Greece's economic and financial situations are worse than before the initial bailout. Greece is in a depression that will continue until either it exits the euro and devalues or it receives continuous transfer payments from the euro zone. The same should be true of Portugal, Spain and Italy as they follow Greece down this slippery slope. By contrast, exiting the euro and devaluing could restore them to prosperity within a couple of years if managed correctly. It was the UK government's ability to borrow from the Bank of England that allowed it to escape going down the same road as Ireland and Spain.

Increasing global competition
Growth requires rising private investment in productive facilities, but private investment in Europe is weak for three reasons.

First, globalisation has added about a billion workers in emerging countries earning low wages by European standards to the global labour force. The growth in investment and production has moved to emerging countries, putting downward pressure on developed country employment and incomes. The cost savings from this movement increased corporate profits and created productivity gains in the national accounts of developed countries. However, they added nothing to their production, employment or worker incomes – so, in effect, they moved output growth from the current-account-deficit countries to the current-account-surplus ones, enlarging global imbalances of saving and investment.

Second, virtually all countries are trying to raise their exports and reduce their imports. Not only is this impossible without a global current-account surplus with Mars, but euro-zone states also have the disadvantage of being linked to Germany, arguably the most competitive country in the world.

Third, small business is the biggest employer. US household deleverage is hurting small business disproportionately, a major factor in the disappointing employment and income growth in this recovery. By contrast, lack of deleverage in the UK has kept employment high relative to output, sacrificing productivity in the process. As a result, real incomes are stable to falling in most developed countries. Add in the tax increases intended to reduce deficits and real disposable incomes are falling more, making sustained GDP growth impossible. Austerity is an additional headwind because it increases the rate of decline in real incomes. As a result, the chances of euro-zone peripheral states achieving sustainable growth without exiting the euro are nil.

Austerity

Most governments spent 10% of national GDP or less in the 1920s; most developed country governments now spend 45–55%. Their soaring spending ran them out of taxing power years ago, so they resorted to deficit financing and have now extended this so far that no developed country government will be able to fulfil all its commitments for age-related spending, entitlements and debt indefinitely. All need to cut their spending – austerity. Government austerity boosts growth when strong private balance sheets enable the sector to pick up the slack and run with it – but that is now impossible.

The fiscal deficits are borrowing investment and consumption from the future – the same as the excessively low interest rates mentioned previously. That future has arrived and austerity must not only end the borrowing from the future, but also repay the borrowing. A lot of research shows small government is better government. Public Choice used US figures from 1929 to 1986 to conclude that maximum productivity growth occurs when government expenditures total about 20% of GDP.

The most efficient way to repay the borrowing could be to radically downsize government by stopping unproductive and wasteful government activity (for example, agricultural and business subsidies) and encouraging the private sector where appropriate. Several small countries – Ireland, New Zealand and some former Soviet states – have done this and prospered. However, this lesson remains unpopular and governments in some countries that downsized successfully, such as Ireland, began growing again, so the less efficient route of depression and default is occurring. Greece, Ireland, Portugal and Spain are showing that austerity without restructuring reduces GDP as fast as or faster than the deficits, condemning them to perpetual deflation and depression.

Chapters 6 and 10 will discuss these issues further, including where and how government ought to intervene in the economy (from both an ethical and an economic point of view). The developed market debt crisis provides an opportunity to reassess and restructure unproductive government activities while preserving those we value most.

Note that the successful restructurings took place when the private sector could take up the slack and run with it. The unsuccessful restructurings are occurring when excess debt is forcing the private sector to delever, so it is unable to take up any slack. This inability means cuts in government spending are lowering GDP by an equal or even greater amount. Chapter 4 will explain why the public and private sector cannot deleverage together, making austerity counterproductive. Subsequent chapters will explain why the most important needs today are government and financial system reform. Unfortunately, government reform is not on anyone's agenda and the powerful bank lobbies are making a mockery of bank reform.

No healthy balance sheet

As mentioned in Chapter 1, the BIS showed the amount of non-financial debt in developed countries is seriously undermining their growth. Chapter 11 will show that emerging country balance sheets are stronger than those of developed countries. Emerging countries account for about half of global GDP, but their combined balance sheets are not nearly strong enough to fund the repair of developed country balance sheets because emerging countries generally have a lower tolerance for debt.

Worse, developed country financial balance sheets are riddled with bad debt, and thus far weaker than non-financial balance sheets. The high debt levels are seriously restricting the number of willing and creditworthy borrowers. Overvalued assets and, especially in Europe, undercapitalisation mean few banks are willing and able lenders. The lack of qualified borrowers and lenders is severely limiting the growth of bank loans to the private sector. The borrowers usually quickly spend the proceeds of these loans on new goods and services. These purchases stimulate the economy and its growth creates demand for more bank loans. Bank loans are high-powered money because the money growth they create stimulates output growth in a virtuous circle – until inflation becomes a problem. By contrast, private-sector deflation is curtailing money growth enough to hurt GDP growth in most developed countries.

The world of computer models does not encompass credit bubbles and bank crises, so banks, bank regulators and central banks can neither see them coming nor adjust to their severity. The bubbles before the Lehman/AIG default were relatively small and their bursting was easily contained. Since none of them created major problems, many banks kept increasing their leverage, up to 50 times net tangible equity and more. Furthermore, many bank balance sheets still contain hidden losses because loans to weak borrowers and securities of distressed governments remain valued at cost until the borrower defaults.

These unrealised losses make many banks technically insolvent and they cannot afford to book losses – even if writing down debts would benefit both the lender and the borrower. They would have significant negative net tangible equity if they had to mark their assets to market, so any default could be catastrophic. They must use their resources to keep their weak borrowers afloat, so cannot lend to borrowers that could use the loans to expand output.

In Spain, for example, efforts have been made to address the value of real-estate assets on banks' balance sheets and sovereign debt holdings (through the European-wide bank stress tests). However, no serious questions have been asked about the quality of corporate loans – even though corporate net income has fallen by 40–60% in Spain and Italy since the financial crisis. The corporate sector's debt-servicing ability has declined sharply, so undercapitalised banks face risks from souring loans in the household, corporate and sovereign sectors – all at the same time.

Central banks are holding interest rates down to increase lending. As previously stated, that is financial repression, which transfers funds from savers to the biggest borrowers, i.e. governments, which in turn curtails investment, productivity and output growth. Worse, several governments have run out of borrowing power and are on life support from international agencies – but international agencies depend on funding from the dwindling number of creditworthy national governments and so are rapidly running out of borrowing power too. As a result, central banks can create only very low-powered money and private-sector debt deflation is negating the record-breaking monetary stimulation in developed countries.

The Minsky moment is approaching

Debt traps are the inability to raise nominal GDP growth above interest rates. They confirm our forefathers' belief that debt is a form of slavery because it eventually dooms nations to depression and/or default. Debt traps have caused sovereign defaults to suddenly soar, often from very low levels, four times since 1800. The first three episodes were in the secondary depressions after wars – in 1837, 1873 and 1931. The fourth was in the early 1980s as a result of:

- unwise borrowing and lending piling up too much debt, especially from foreign creditors;
- weak revenues and poor credit histories creating rollover risk;
- soaring debt costs owing to short-term borrowing in a period of rising interest rates.

The rapid rise in defaults in all four cases indicates that the causative factors do not accrue linearly but accumulate below the surface until a tipping point has been passed. Unwise borrowing, overindebtedness and weak revenues currently affect a large number of countries, so rising interest rates would cause a rash of defaults among those with poor credit histories. The subprime mortgage fiasco sparked a banking crisis in 2007. Banking crises are far more common than sovereign debt defaults, especially by developed countries, which have a much better credit history than emerging ones.

The cluster of defaults in small countries did not affect the global economy or major financial markets greatly in the early 1980s because the finances of the major nations were sound and their banks well-capitalised. However, the budget adjustments major countries must make to stabilise their debt-to-GDP ratios at acceptable levels are as great as or greater than those required by emerging countries. Furthermore, austerity is putting the cart before the horse – shrinking GDP and threatening increasing defaults that their undercapitalised banking systems will not be able to withstand. The proper first step is to recapitalise the banking system. Failure to do so could spread a fiscal and banking crisis in peripheral Europe to all states with either sovereign debt problems or undercapitalised banking systems – a pretty inclusive list, so debt traps will probably engulf many more countries before optimal global growth is achieved.

This time really is different because there is no balance sheet big enough and strong enough to fund the need to recapitalise the banks and write off the bad debt. Instead, massive amounts of new debt have been created in an effort to solve the problems created by too much debt. This must be a new high in collective insanity. Funding the resulting outsized fiscal deficits is consuming saving, thereby aggravating the already huge global current-account imbalances (see Chapter 4). Worse, it is inviting sovereign defaults and debt traps.

Fiscal stimulation has gone into reverse and monetary stimulation shows few signs of raising growth or inflation rates. As a result, rising debt-to-GDP ratios are likely to create a cluster of defaults. Worse, the cluster is likely to include too-big-to-bail-out banks and governments unless they start to take their debt problems more seriously, or the rise of another as yet unseen long-term cycle offsets the strong deflationary force of the current credit cycle. This chapter has detailed the challenges the authorities are facing. The next chapter explains why their policies have failed.

4

Policy errors

When credit was limited, financial markets disciplined borrowers by refusing to lend to those lacking adequate collateral and income to pay the interest and repay the loan – so few governments could borrow much under the gold standard. They began to break the golden fetters at the Genoa Conference in 1922 and continued to do so until President Nixon ended all limits to credit by closing the gold window in 1971. Unlimited credit enabled both extreme financial repression (see Chapter 3) and the Eurasian savings glut, a gigantic vendor-financing scheme whereby currency manipulation by mercantilist save-and-export countries to increase their exports funded consumption in borrow-and-spend ones.

Financial repression and vendor financing caused negative real short-term rates and a strong downward trend in real long-term interest rates (see Figure 3), which, in turn, misallocated capital into housing booms and soaring government deficits. Governments were the main beneficiaries of the easing credit. They spent 10% or less of GDP in peacetime before 1923 compared with up to 55% in recent years. Deficit financing and money printing created inflation – a huge hidden tax that enabled governments to wrest up to about half of GDP from the private sector without

Figure 3   **30-year Treasury inflation-protected securities**
Yield, %

Sources: Federal Reserve; Lombard Street Research

inciting civil unrest. In his book, *Civilization: The West and the Rest*,[3] Niall Ferguson explains the six institutional requirements he regards as critical to national success:

1 Competitiveness
2 Cutting-edge science/technology
3 Property-owning democracy
4 Modern medicine
5 Mass markets
6 Saving and investment

Credit restrictions enhanced the returns from producing goods and services because they allocated funds to those who could make the best use of them. Keen competition and high saving and investment produced fast growth rates, rapid innovation and high productivity. Mass markets boomed, raising every-one's living standards. By contrast, modern financial engineering insidiously changed economic and financial conditions from favouring production to favouring speculation in asset prices, and in so doing drove property prices up far faster than incomes rose, eroding point 3. In addition, Chapter 3 showed that lower than warranted interest rates reduce the quality of investment and balance sheets. This reduces competitiveness, so low interest rates erode points 6 and 1 directly. Lower-quality investment plus lack of competitiveness reduces research and innovation and the ability to create mass markets, i.e. points 2 and 5 indirectly and, eventually, point 4.

Although fiat money enables unlimited credit, its long-term viability depends on interest rates yielding a premium over inflation. Central banks lower interest rates below the rate of inflation to move production and consumption from the future to the present. This ploy works as long as enough creditworthy borrowers are willing to borrow and enough banks possess sufficient capital and reserves to keep lending. However, overuse of the ploy has so reduced the number of both willing and able borrowers and willing and able lenders that the current excessively low interest rates are having the following four counterproductive effects on the economy and financial markets:

- They are depleting the incomes and net worth of savers (for the benefit of banks and speculators), so are acting as a hidden tax on saving and slowing growth.
- They are signalling deflation is on the horizon, so encouraging the hoarding of cash that is helping to bring on the deflation.
- The bubbles in risk assets they created have now burst and are

forcing private-sector deleverage – although low-powered money has pushed US equities to a post-Great Recession peak.
- They are creating distrust of financial institutions and markets.

The average real short interest rate has been about 2% over the past couple of centuries and the real long rate about 2¾%. Most central banks in developed countries are trying to generate an inflation rate of about 2%, so sustainable fiat money would need 4% policy rates and 4¾% long-term sovereign rates. Rates that high would cause severe repercussions in most developed country economies, proving they are basically insolvent and remain functional only through excess liquidity.

Worse, the excess liquidity keeps piling up debt, which is already excessive, so the credit system must ultimately collapse in the absence of a fundamental restructuring in both government and the financial industry. Central banks have greatly increased doubt about the continuing viability of fiat money with their massive monetary stimulation, which has driven risk-free interest rates far below inflation rates. Money supply growth followed the rises in monetary bases until the Lehman/AIG default in 2009.

Then a funny thing happened on the way to the printing presses. The coefficient of correlation between the combined monetary bases and money supplies in the US, the euro zone and Japan fell from 0.64 before the default to 0.04 after (see Figure 4). Central banks accounted for about two-thirds of the variation in money supplies before the default and for none since. Instead, lack of capital and hidden losses on their balance sheets are preventing banks from extending fresh credit, even though they have plenty of reserves.

As we will see later, the enormous difficulty in engineering

Figure 4   **Growth in monetary base and money supply**
            Annual growth, %

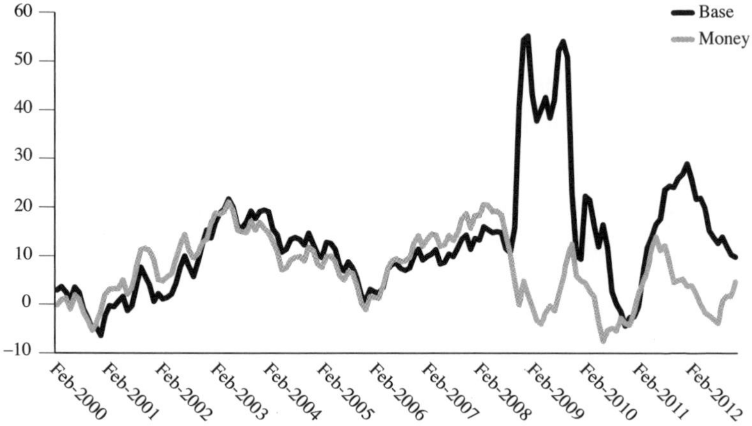

Sources: Bank of Japan; European Central Bank; Federal Reserve; Lombard Street Research

even minor banking reform means the looming European sovereign debt/banking crisis will cause severe damage to the credit structure. At present, lack of capital is forcing European banks to reduce their loans, so growth in the combined money supplies of the US, the euro zone and Japan has fallen to just 2%. Banks need capital to lend. The US has done the most bank recapitalisation and is leading a recovery in credit growth, but the euro zone is unable to participate without massive bank recapitalisations. Bond markets are far closer to the money-printing process than stock markets, and the flight of funds from risk assets reduced intermediate and long-term yields on the highest-quality sovereign bonds significantly.

That drop to extremely low sovereign yields in the face of falling money supplies shows the great advantage unlimited credit bestows on those involved in and close to the money creation process – governments, politicians, bankers, developers and speculators. Unlimited credit has turned companies inventing, making and distributing goods and services into playthings for financial engineers. Those who borrowed most to buy out competitors profited most, so competition dwindled. Fiscal deficits have usurped saving from investment, so innovation and productivity have fallen. Living standards rose for the few close to money creation, but fell for the private producers of goods and services. Meanwhile, the Eurasian savings glut created massive global imbalances of saving and investment that must be corrected.

Financial balances

Most economists and financial analysts devour income statements and neglect balance sheets, which yield equally important information. Every credit creates a corresponding debit and vice versa, so their sums always equal zero – saving equals investment, for example. In the national balance sheet, the sum of household and business (private), government (public) and foreign (capital account) saving must equal domestic investment. Saving less investment equals the financial balance. The private-sector financial balance plus the public-sector financial balance equals the capital account. A negative sum of the domestic financial balances imports an equal amount of foreign saving with a capital-account surplus – the automatic result of a current-account deficit. A positive sum of the domestic financial balances exports an equal amount of domestic saving with a capital-account deficit – the automatic result of a current-account surplus.

Table 1 shows the US current-account deficits for 2007 and 2010 with the sign changed to show the capital imports equal to the negative domestic financial balances. The small differences between the totals and the current accounts result from measuring errors in the national accounts.

Table 1 **US current-account deficits, $ billion**

	Private saving	Private investment	Public saving	Public investment	Total	Current account
2007	514	−829	−233	−165	−713	716
2010	1,245	−255	−1,299	−171	−480	479

Most people believe that chronic current-account deficits are bad, but they never cause problems if: (1) the foreign desire to invest in the country equals or exceeds that country's desire to import goods and services; and (2) the capital imports fund the expansion of productive facilities. The increased production generates the additional income needed to pay the interest on the rising debts. Unfortunately, the second condition is seldom met. Capital imports usually fund government largesse and/or private consumption, so chronic current-account deficits end up damaging the economy and financial structure. This has occurred many times in Latin America, caused the subprime mortgage crisis in the US, and is causing government and bank insolvency in the peripheral states of Europe.

Every import is another country's export, so global current-account surpluses must equal global current-account deficits. The key point about the Eurasian savings glut is that the save-and-export countries can pile up surpluses for ever, but the borrow-and-spend countries eventually run out of the ability to pay the interest on their rising debts. The vendor-financing scheme collapses when the debtors in borrow-and-spend countries fail to pay the interest on their debts, greatly reducing the value of the accumulated surpluses.

The US subprime mortgage crisis ended the biggest such scheme in history. In addition, the highest debt-to-income ratios in history guaranteed that this collapse would invoke the worst financial and economic repercussions ever. Current-account surplus countries will suffer as much as or more than deficit ones. Chinese and Japanese current-account surpluses together amassed almost half of the $10 trillion of global international reserves. The collapse of the vendor-financing scheme was the most important factor in their huge annual surpluses disappearing, although other factors are contributing to the halving of the Chinese trend growth rate, which will affect much of Asia.

Developed country governments took advantage of the subprime financial crisis to extend their powers over the private sector, casually tossing centuries of classic capitalist practices along with constitutional and contract law into the dustbin of history in the process. However, all their efforts to stimulate growth have been in vain. Annual US growth since the end of the housing bubble has been virtually zero. Europe, the area with the highest debt ratios, has suffered even more. The public debt of many European countries is so high that they cannot rescue and recapitalise their banks. Instead, the need for private deleverage is forcing banks to intermediate saving into fiscal deficits – making the banking system dysfunctional and output growth impossible.

European authorities are handling this unique condition badly. Table 1 showed that changes in foreign financial balances offset changes in US domestic financial balances. The euro-zone monetary union prevents the capital surpluses of the save-and-export euro-zone states funding the current-account deficits of the borrow-and-spend ones, so euro-zone current-account imbalances keep accumulating. The European authorities are imposing austerity – increased public saving – on peripheral states at the same time as forcing banks to raise vast amounts of equity (although not enough to rectify their balance sheet problems) – i.e. increase saving in the hope the added saving would help lower and eventually eliminate their current-account deficits.

That policy cannot work. Increased public saving will reduce GDP by as much as or more than public saving because private investment cannot take up the slack. Lack of competitiveness and intense global competition make greatly reducing current-account deficits impossible and the moribund domestic economy cannot support increased investment. As a result, the only possible outcome of austerity is shrinking investment and output – i.e. depression. Worse, European banks are weapons of mass financial destruction.

Governments and banks

Governments did their best to thwart most of the long-overdue correction in asset prices by rushing in to protect banks during the Great Recession, guaranteeing their liabilities and bailing out failing financial and non-financial institutions. This temporarily reversed the inability to meet liabilities and consequent fall in asset prices, but the reprieve is only temporary. Transferring bad private debt onto public balance sheets simply lets zombie companies compete with more productive companies, thus postponing

Figure 5   **European banks: price-to-book values**

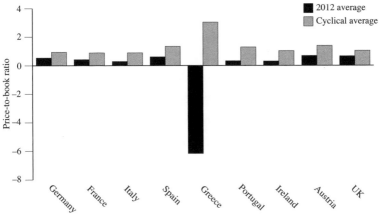

Source: Datastream

Figure 6   **Fall in book value reflected in 2012 average PB ratio (versus cyclical average), %**

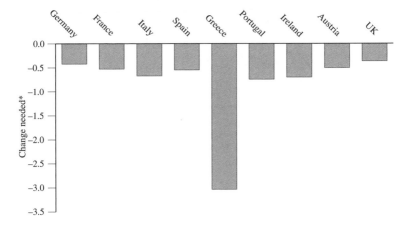

*Change in book value needed to return the current price-to-book ratio to its 7½-year average.
Source: Datastream

the necessary corrections of imbalances while making them more costly in the long run.

European banks are grossly undercapitalised, riddled with bad debt and have shockingly big loan books relative to their deposit bases. In addition, markets have recognised the threats the still-inflated values of sovereign debt and loan collateral for both household and business debt pose to banks. As a result, price-to-book (PB) values across the European banking system are at rock-bottom levels compared with their seven-and-a-half-year averages. They imply banks will suffer losses ranging between 50% and 95% from the book values of their assets (see Figures 5 and 6). Financial markets often underestimate or exaggerate potential losses. Spanish bank prices implied the smallest losses in the spring of 2012 and were the next to need bailouts, so most banks will probably end up at the higher end of the range.

The European Banking Authority (EBA) has attempted to address the risks sovereign debt holdings pose to bank solvency in the euro zone. It calculated the value of each bank's euro-zone sovereign portfolio at September 2011 market prices – only scratching the surface of banks' balance sheets. The amounts of capital required to reach the mandated 9% Tier 1 capital ratio under this exercise are shown by country in Chart 7. As part of the October 2011 bailout, €48 billion was made available to recapitalise the Greek banks through the European Financial Stability Facility (EFSF). The banks received a €25 billion capital injection through the EFSF in April 2012 and the remainder followed the December 2012 Greek debt buy-back.

Spanish banks faced both a large capital shortfall based on sovereign debt holdings and substantial question marks over the poor quality of real-estate loan books. The latter has been addressed

Figure 7   **European banks: capital shortfall, September 2011**
€ *billion*

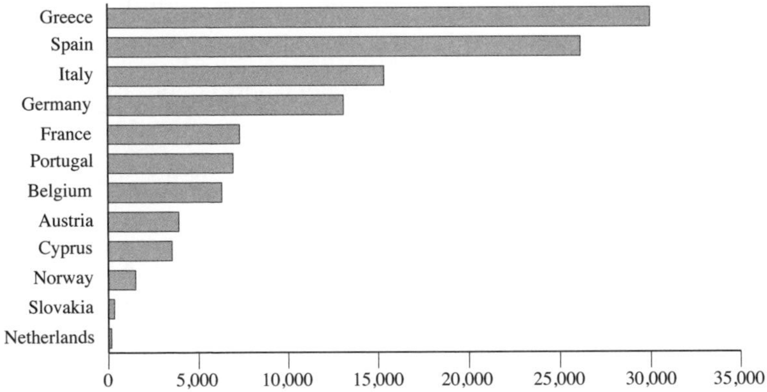

Sources: European Banking Authority

by a separate round of national stress tests and €100 billion was made available to the Spanish government to recapitalise its banks; €37 billion of European Stability Mechanism (ESM) bonds was used to recapitalise four Spanish banks and €2.5 billion to recapitalise the national Asset Management Company. The latest Greek and Spanish recapitalisation plans both include a degree of private-sector involvement – share sales to private investors for the former, losses for preference shareholders for the latter – as the EU appetite to provide public bailout funds wanes. Moreover, if €48 billion is an accurate amount of capital needed by Greek banks (and this figure may well prove inadequate), the true capital needs for Spain and Italy (with banking sectors several times the size of Greece's) will be many times larger.

The euro-zone banks were, on the whole, able to meet the 9% Tier 1 capital ratio by September 2012, with the exception of some Cypriot banks and Italy's Monte dei Paschi, facing a €1.5 billion shortfall (before taking into account the likely poor state of the bank's domestic loan book), but the results of the exercise are fairly meaningless. Little has been done to get to grips with the true state of euro-zone bank balance sheets and, even when black holes are found, no one feels any urgency to address them with the euro zone's immediate liquidity problems soothed by central bank funding.

The ECB specifically designed long-term repo operations to encourage the banks in peripheral states to load up on their own sovereign debt. They reinforced the euro-zone Ponzi scheme of insolvent banks supporting the insolvent sovereigns that were guaranteeing the liabilities of the insolvent banks. However, this did nothing to alleviate the credit squeeze on the private sector as banks funding government deficits rob business of funding, especially small business, which relies exclusively on banks for funding. The June 2012 agreement to allow the ESM to recapitalise banks directly was intended to break this link between the sovereigns and the banks – another euro-zone farce, given that the ESM derives its creditworthiness from the governments in the first place. Policymakers have since reintroduced the idea that domestic governments will have to share some of the burden of bank recapitalisations alongside the ESM – a futile exercise.

Indeed, the crisis-fighting institutions in the euro zone are seriously lacking. The proposed bank regulator is mired in a sea of discord, and looming losses have quelled creditor country appetites for the euro-zone bank deposit guarantee necessary to escape from the bank runs out of peripheral states – because it would mutualise responsibility for failing banks. The ESM has been approved by euro-zone member states and ratified by the German constitutional court, but its €500 billion lending capacity remains woefully inadequate and serious disagreement remains over whether the fund can carry out primary market bond purchases. The snail's pace at which euro-zone decision-making proceeds means it would be difficult to boost the ESM's capacity in an emergency, and policymakers have shown a persistent reluctance to deploy funds that have already been approved.

Recapitalising banks is deflationary

European banks must raise their equity ratios to cover the potential losses on assets with market values below book values. Even the EBA-mandated increase in Tier 1 capital from 6% to 9% of risk-weighted assets is insufficient to make the euro-zone banking system resilient to the rigours of simultaneous public and private deleverage. Their balance sheets are so bad that a lack of investors in bank equity is forcing European banks to reduce their lending in both European and non-European markets. Funding government deficits is barely offsetting the drop in the money supply caused by liquidating bank loans. Loan contraction forces households and small and medium-sized enterprises, which have no alternative source of funding, to spend less and save more, thereby lowering demand growth in the economy.

Worse, European banks are the main source of global trade credit, so their loan contraction will hurt global trade as in 2008–09. Continuing contraction of bank lending will cause deflation – but recapitalising the banks is deflationary too. Investors in bank equity would pay for their purchases of equity by drawing down their deposits. However, the bank enters the transaction on its books as increases in cash and capital, so does not create an off-setting deposit. As a result, the money supply falls by the amount of capital raised.

Shrinking bank balance sheets is strongly deflationary. According to Olivier Sarkozy, head of global financial services at the Carlyle Group, Europe's banking sector has $55 trillion of assets, four times larger than the US's. European banks also have $30 trillion of wholesale deposits (ten times more than US banks) and need to roll over $800 billion monthly. The far greater size of the European banking system, its higher leverage of net tangible equity and its dependency on wholesale funding (large temporary deposits, mostly from companies and other financial institutions that may quickly disappear) make Sarkozy's estimate that it needs $2 trillion of additional capital look conservative.

The probability of European banks being able to raise $2 trillion of capital is zero. Bank recapitalisation requires real saving – not funny money. Households normally account for most saving, so bank recapitalisation ultimately depletes household incomes through a combination of higher taxes, artificially low interest rates and increased bank charges. A $2 trillion or more hit to European incomes is out of the question. As a result, European banks will be shrinking their balance sheets over the intermediate term.

Private borrowing is the mechanism that turns bank reserves into money, but creditworthy borrowers that are willing to borrow are becoming an ever more endangered species, as financial and economic conditions deteriorate. Small business remains mired in the Great Recession while many households face falling real incomes and are trying to repay loans, so few are either willing or able to borrow. Their desperate need for capital makes banks that are willing and able to lend an even rarer species.

Figure 8 **Euro-zone M3**
€ *billion*

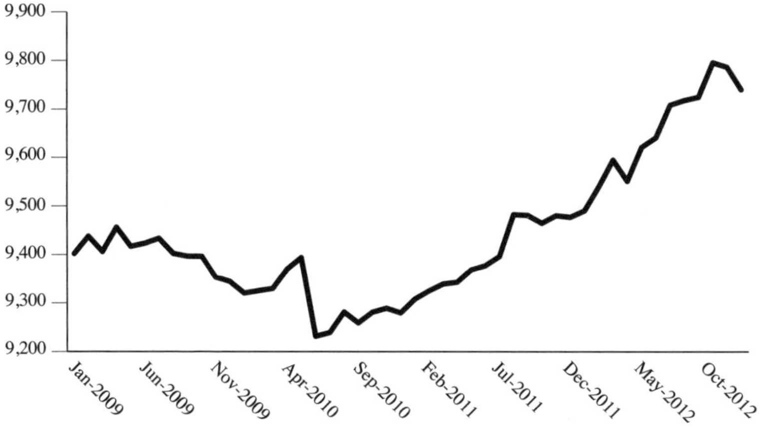

Sources: European Central Bank; Lombard Street Research

The banks' traditional moneymaking machine cannot function until household, small business and bank balance sheets are
repaired. Capital constraints on banks and borrower caution on
adding new debt prevent the massive excess bank reserves being
held in central banks from becoming loans and creating money.
This means the excess bank reserves central banks are creating
by monetising government debt cannot increase either money
or output growth. By contrast, ECB purchases of illiquid sovereign debt did help the euro-zone recovery reverse the decline
in M3 caused by the Great Recession and the deflationary effect
of repairing bank balance sheets (see Figure 8). These purchases
stopped as the ECB took in more sovereign bonds as collateral.
Outright monetary transactions, announced in September 2012,
dramatically reduced periphery yields but will not create new

money until activated. The combination of imposed austerity and trying to repair bank balance sheets has crippled peripheral Europe.

The euro-zone Ponzi scheme

Euro-zone debt is estimated to be 443% of GDP, the third-highest in the world behind the UK and Japan but far above the US at 355%. High debt levels are completely unmanageable in a currency union burdened with a one-size-fits-none monetary policy and a lack of both comprehensive deposit insurance and fiscal transfers. In addition, insolvent European banks sold a lot of credit insurance. They probably will not be able to fulfil their commitments when defaults start piling up insurance claims. Significant private or public defaults and/or a national exit from the euro would cause a European banking crisis. Portugal, Ireland and Spain are the leading candidates for the latter, with Italy not far behind.

Euro-zone austerity combined with excessive leverage, negative demographics, the rising cost of age-related entitlements, expanding global competition and nominal GDP growth below interest rates have made the policy of funding more debt until peripheral Europe can grow out of debt problems impossible. Being in the euro eliminates nominal currency devaluation, the usual palliative to lack of competitiveness and debt problems. Core states are aggravating the situation further by trying to rule out sovereign defaults too, pushing Greece, Portugal, Ireland and Spain into deep depressions with no relief in sight. Italy and several smaller countries are sliding down the same slippery slope. Unsurprisingly, money and people are fleeing those countries in droves.

There is not enough money on the planet to keep bailing out insolvent European governments and banks for ever. Growing and/or inflating out of their debt problems are impossible. The EFSF, its successor the ESM and even the IMF can only postpone the inevitable defaults. Greece has already proved two things:

- The bailouts are merely increasing the losses when the defaults occur. Eurobonds would not be any better – borrowing cannot solve the problem of too much debt.
- Defaulting within the euro solves nothing because lack of competitiveness dooms peripheral states to depression without continual transfer payments.

Adequate transfer payments are very unlikely, so the peripheral states face long periods of wage cuts and high unemployment. The alternative is to negotiate the redenomination of their foreign-held euro liabilities into their local currency and leave the euro. Unsuitable members leaving the euro is not a problem. Ultimately, that is the only way the euro can survive, yet Greece voted to remain in the euro – even though so-called bailouts and its default placed it in a considerably worse financial and economic condition than prevailed before its first bailout. This spectacular failure indicates no exit will occur until every other option has failed and the costs of maintaining the status quo have risen by orders of magnitude. This obstinacy puts the survival of the euro in doubt.

Furthermore, government intervention in the Greek default has cast doubt on the value of credit default swaps (CDS) to hedge sovereign risk. Asset prices are floating on an ocean of credit. The global debt-to-GDP ratio has probably quadrupled from the levels in the early 1980s. The resulting high debt ratios have increased the risk of default exponentially, so the ability to appropriately hedge risk is crucial to prevent losses from collapsing the credit structure. The Greek-inspired fear that CDSs no longer hedge sovereign debt properly should have lowered investor demand for weak sovereign debt, but ECB activities and the ban on shorting European sovereign debt unless it is a direct hedge have masked the effect on yields. Greece, Portugal, Ireland and Spain probably will not emerge from their bailouts and Italy is likely to fall into the same predicament.

The peripheral states suffer solvency not liquidity problems, so reliance on the ECB to maintain the status quo while the politicians dither over inadequate measures to counter bank runs on the notoriously undercapitalised European banks should cause significant failures. Enormous ECB liquidity injections, through both long-term repurchase agreements and emergency loan assistance, have kept insolvent banks afloat. However, insolvent banks must shrink their balance sheets. Sovereign debt does not entail risk-weighted capital, so the long-term repurchase agreements enabled capital-constrained banks in peripheral states to buy the bonds of their governments to use as collateral for loans from the ECB and earn interest rate spreads that will increase their profits and add to their capital.

However, loan losses are eroding their capital. They must keep shrinking their loan books, so the massive ECB liquidity injections have barely kept money growth positive. Banks have so little use for this money that even periphery banks have started to pay back long-term refinancing operation (LTRO) money. The monetary base grew by almost half in the year to August 2012, while M3 grew by a mere 2½%. Worse, the amounts of bad sovereign debt on the balance sheets of banks in peripheral states are rising rapidly and the recovery rate may be small. Moreover, peripheral euro-zone governments either have run out or are running out of the ability to borrow, so they have no chance of being able to honour their bank deposit guarantees. European banks must also shrink the yawning gap of loans over deposits in the context of runs on banks in peripheral states – not a pretty picture.

The Eurosystem consists of the ECB and the central banks of the member states that have adopted the euro as their official currency. Each national central bank (NCB) does all the day-to-day transactions with its domestic commercial banks and settles its country's participation in international transactions in the pan-European Target-2 payments system. Target-2 records the net position of each NCB with all other NCBs at the ECB in real time. This system concentrates the lower-quality collateral in peripheral NCBs, especially through the emergency liquidity assistance (ELA) programme, which accepts lower-quality collateral to relieve liquidity problems, such as the effects of bank runs. Fear of exiting the euro and having bank deposits redenominated into heavily discounted national currencies instead of euros has caused runs on banks in peripheral states.

The Eurosystem made no allowance for exits from the euro or sovereign defaults. This was a serious error, as it gave rise to an implicit assumption that no NCB could ever default, so no one considered deposit imbalances would be a problem. The ELA programme offers almost unlimited funding with virtually any collateral – effectively removing credit monitoring from the banking system. As a result, persistent debit balances (that in bank-to-bank transactions would have caused credit to be cut off) created massive accumulations of liabilities that otherwise would never have been permitted.

Bank runs were a major factor (current-account deficits are usually ultimately funded outside the banking system) in core states involuntarily amassing credits of almost €1 trillion to offset peripheral state liabilities in Target-2 in April 2012, about one-third of the entire ECB balance sheet and over 60% of total deposits. Determining the sizes of these runs is difficult because Spaniards moving deposits from Spain to Germany do not show up in euro-zone statistics; they remain Spanish euro deposits. They do show up as a Bank of Spain debit and a Bundesbank credit in Target-2 – but netted with every other private and public transaction between Spain and Germany.

The NCB's liabilities are its government's liabilities, so Target-2 is strengthening the links between sovereign and bank credit in the European Ponzi scheme of insolvent banks supporting the insolvent governments that are guaranteeing the liabilities of the insolvent banks. Ever-increasing ECB liquidity injections are compounding the imbalances, not reducing them. Even if a bank run could be halted immediately upon a country deciding to exit the euro, the exit would still decimate the recovery value of its liabilities at the ECB. Creditors always pay when debtors borrow too much and the NCBs holding the offsetting credits will have to write them down correspondingly. Germany is against mutualising public-sector debt, yet Target-2 has been mutualising private debt since the European crisis began.

Markets will react violently when they discover this, but Target-2 is not the problem. The problem is grossly overlevered sovereigns and commercial banks. Markets had priced in realistic risks of sovereign defaults and bank failures, but a statement by the ECB's president, Mario Draghi, that the bank would do 'whatever it takes to save the euro' calmed investor fears – even though it was a bluff because the ECB cannot provide the most needed element to save the euro: bank capital. Several countries are losing patience with the current policies and any one of them can force another default by vetoing a payment under one of the bailout agreements. The banks (except in Cyprus, which was forced to seek bailouts) survived the Greek default, but the private sectors in some peripheral states have even worse financial problems than their governments.

The rapidly rising credits and debits in the Target-2 system indicate a pressing need for a change in European policy. Greece's 70% default on its privately held debt after €240 billion of bailouts, followed by a further restructuring in December 2012, shows that the unnecessary deferral of debt write-downs is:

- rapidly escalating the long-term costs of deleverage;
- seriously delaying Europe's return to healthy growth;
- heaping intolerable losses on creditor country taxpayers;
- pushing Europe into depression.

That the Greek default did not change European policy one iota proves an overriding agenda. The only agenda that can justify continuing the current policies is that the German government considers monetary union a mere stepping-stone to fiscal union – but only after it is satisfied with peripheral states' commitment to financial rectitude. It apparently does not realise that Target-2 is busy creating a de facto fiscal union lacking any fiscal safeguards whatsoever. Nor do the citizens in the peripheral states, who would welcome greater centralisation because they despise the corruption in their governments and hope encroachment on their sovereignty will greatly reduce it. In the absence of significant policy changes, the cost of 'preserving the euro at all costs' will be a European Great Depression.

Greece has been in a depression for five years and clearly exhibits what may happen in Ireland, Portugal, Spain, Italy and other countries as the depression spreads. Imports of goods and services are likely to diminish greatly because few will have the money to pay for them. Trade credit could dry up and suppliers could suspend shipments through fear of non-payment. Tax revenue is plummeting as incomes fall, and those that can pay delay in the hope that they can pay later with the greatly discounted national currency.

For some, devaluation and default may become the only option to escape the prospect of years of depression, high unemployment and being dictated to by creditor governments. Creditor governments themselves cannot escape the pain of depression on their doorstep and may eventually reject throwing good money after bad to bail out their neighbours – although, as the Target-2 discussion showed, it is already far too late. Creditors will pay one way or another (through a decade of poor growth and eroding asset values, or through a severe sovereign credit event and euro exits).

It's deflation, stupid

Chapter 3 explained that debt traps have caused soaring sovereign defaults and deflation in the past and are about to do so again.

Several European countries are caught in debt traps. They will have to restructure their financial institutions to eliminate systemic risk, and reform their labour markets and downsize their government to achieve competitiveness in global markets – but structural reform is not on anyone's agenda. Worse, big countries are downplaying the threats posed by monumental fiscal deficits and soaring debt-to-GDP ratios. For example, the US Congressional Budget Office conjured up a budget with pie-in-the-sky figures, such as a 26% rise in personal and a 27% rise in corporate income tax receipts in 2013 – all from 2.6% nominal GDP growth. This budget also predicted GDP will grow faster in the next decade than in the last one, even though credit liquidation and the ageing population will undoubtedly lower growth.

The prospects of unending massive fiscal deficits and money printing as well as soaring bank reserves have kindled almost universal fears of inflation, even hyperinflation, but they are misplaced for five reasons:

- Most important from a long-term point of view, the losses from falling asset prices and the need for serial bank recapitalisations make credit liquidation deflationary.
- Moving private debt onto public balance sheets does nothing to reduce losses. A simple, but strangely overlooked fact is that governments garner all their revenues from the private sector. If the private sector is overburdened with debt, the whole nation is overburdened with debt.
- Bank reserves are not money. Figure 4 showed that huge increases in monetary bases do not necessarily result in money supply growth. As noted above, the deflationary forces of undercapitalised banks and private-sector deleverage severed the link between the monetary

Figure 9   **Japanese M2**
             ¥ *trillion*

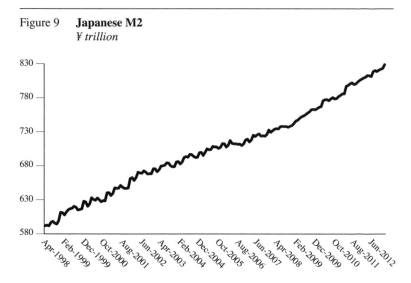

Sources: Bank of Japan; Lombard Street Research

base and money supply. In late 2008 and early 2009, the combined
money supply growth in the US, Japan and the euro zone fell as
growth in the combined monetary base soared from an annual rate
of 10% to almost 50%. The pattern in 2011 was similar.

- A growing money supply does not guarantee inflation. Figure 9
  shows that Japanese money supply kept growing during its decades
  of deflation.

- Disaster awaits the euro zone. It needs either to create a credible
  and persuasive path towards union or to break up. The alternative is
  a true lost decade of zero growth at best, high unemployment and
  intolerable welfare losses for the populations of the most indebted
  countries. Calls for more union from politicians and pundits are
  coinciding with the members drifting apart, so break-up is the more
  likely outcome.

Of course, Europe does not have a monopoly on insolvent banks. However, its banks have less capital and bigger differentials between their book and mark-to-market values, so they now pose significantly more systemic risk than banks in other countries. Like others, euro-zone states guarantee their bank deposits and fund deficiencies from bank failures by selling bonds. However, countries that cannot sell bonds in financial markets apply for bailouts – to be able to borrow from the bailout mechanisms, first the EFSF and then the ESM, which sell bonds in financial markets to raise the funds they lend. The solvent euro-zone states guarantee the EFSF and ESM bonds, so are liable for all the losses. Northern Europe's overemphasis on austerity is its way of trying to limit the losses.

Soaring sovereign debt burdens and more bailout recipients are reducing the number of creditworthy guarantors of the EFSF and ESM debts, so they have been downgraded – probably not for the last time. The costs of bailing out rise as the ratings of the EFSF and ESM fall in line with those of their guarantors – threatening a downward spiral in ratings. Egan Jones, the only major lender-pay ratings company (borrower-pay ratings companies tend to follow it), downgraded Germany to A+ and kept it on watch for further downgrades because of the big potential losses on credits to peripheral states. As explained above, austerity is counterproductive, so the euro-zone elite are trying to spread their liability across the globe through more IMF participation in the bailout mechanism. Understandably, this idea has had a cool reception, so this contingent liability weighs ever more heavily on the remaining highly rated countries.

The proposals to create a bank regulator, deposit insurance and bank guarantees have slowed the bank runs in peripheral states. However, these measures address relative solvency risks but not devaluation risks, as they cannot preserve the euro value of domestic deposits in countries that might exit the euro. The German proposal to issue euro-zone bonds backed by the gold reserves of the borrowing country is the only one so far that would ease the solvency squeeze on peripheral states. Gold-backed bonds would have low interest rates and, depending on the details of the scheme and gold prices, could cover more than a trivial amount of peripheral state needs, but this is nowhere near enough to cover both their fiscal deficits and their bank runs.

The only way to avert the dismal scenario of a euro-zone sovereign debt/banking crisis is full fiscal and political union. This would enable Eurobonds, the nationalisation of all banks, the identification and write-off of all losses, followed by the recapitalisation and, ultimately, reprivatisation of banks, but the negotiations to bring this about would take decades. There is more evidence of countries drifting apart – such as wide differences between Angela Merkel's and François Hollande's solutions for the euro zone and the UK preparing to pull out of almost all areas of justice and home affairs, perhaps even the EU itself – than of them coming closer together.

People believe the ESM will recapitalise peripheral state banks as their governments lack the debt capacity. However, the ESM will not have sufficient funding authority to do this and agreement to extend that authority adequately is unlikely. With sufficient pan-euro-zone funding to recapitalise the banks not forthcoming, the only other option for heavily indebted governments is to exit the euro, renegotiate their euro liabilities into the national currency and print the money needed to recapitalise their banks. This would be extremely painful, but far less painful than

Figure 10   **US money market funds: % change in exposure, May 2011–January 2013**

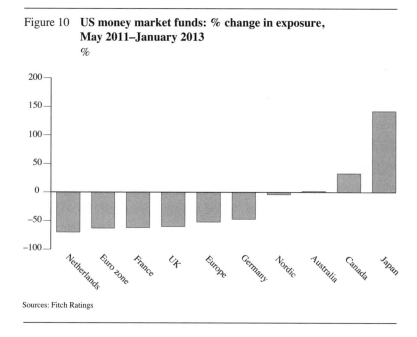

Sources: Fitch Ratings

the looming sovereign defaults and resulting collapse of European banks within the euro, which is likely without a substantial increase in ESM borrowing capacity and a willingness of creditor countries and the ECB to pay rather than just say 'whatever it takes'.

Even so, German yields remain at or below similar-term US yields – a puzzling situation with German contingent liabilities escalating with each new development in the euro zone – so European money has moved to the US. Furthermore, US money market funds (MMF) reduced their overall exposure to European banks in 2011 and 2012, replacing it with increased exposures to Australia, Canada, Japan and US Treasuries and agency paper (see Figure 10), even though they increased European holdings in the months after the ECB announced unlimited purchase of conforming peripheral debt. This funding accounted for about 4% of short-term liabilities among European banks.

The Fed initially eased the consequent shortage of dollars in Europe with swap agreements with several central banks to keep the dollar down, but the cost of borrowing dollars in exchange for euros remained elevated until the ECB's LTROs eased liquidity fears in euro-zone markets and made investors more willing to lend dollars. Nonetheless, dollar liquidity cannot offset euro deleverage.

The long and deep recession that has begun in Europe will cause soaring private-sector defaults; 25% of euro-zone listed non-financial companies made a loss in 2012. Neither European banks nor the bailout mechanisms are equipped to handle the combination of inadequate bank capitalisation, shrinking wholesale funding, bank runs in peripheral states and rising defaults. A European sovereign debt/banking crisis would keep Europe in a long depression. The big question is how much global damage it would cause.

Chapter 2 explained that current financial conditions are unique because household, business and government balance sheets are all overextended in most developed countries, so there is no balance sheet to fund economic growth while the others go through their required contractions. It also explained that the following six steps are required to grow and/or inflate out of debt crises:

- recapitalise the banks to enable sustained loan growth;
- reduce government spending;
- reform labour policies to lower unit labour costs;
- devalue the currency to enable net export growth;

- increase private investment;
- stabilise the housing market.

Chapter 3 showed that all seven factors that facilitated previous exits from debt crises have been headwinds since the 2007–08 banking crisis. As a result, in the euro zone:

- banks are shrinking loans;
- governments are raising taxes;
- workers are rioting against change, so unit labour costs remain too high;
- national currency devaluation is impossible;
- private investment is shrinking;
- slow progress in tackling the overhang of bad real-estate loans is preventing the stabilisation of housing.

No euro-zone country has shown the slightest flicker of comprehension that there was a credit bubble that has burst and the era of continuous borrowing from the future with excess debt creation is over, or that reducing costs with austerity cannot substitute for reducing costs by devaluation. As a result, the lists above show that reality on the ground is the exact reverse of what is needed to grow and/or inflate out of the debt crisis. Furthermore, the 'bailouts' are merely raising public-sector debt in countries that could not pay the interest on their outstanding debt before the bailouts. As a result, debt burdens are spiralling out of control.

Peripheral states never recovered from the Great Recession. Global conditions and the imposition of austerity have removed any reasonable prospect of them doing so in the foreseeable future. Those receiving bailouts can keep servicing their debts

only with the quarterly unanimous authorisation of funds by 27
countries plus the IMF. Authorisation theoretically depends on
meeting budget deficit to GDP ratio targets. However, doing so is
impossible because falling GDP keeps raising the ratio as fast as
or faster than reduced deficits lower it – the major reason Greece
defaulted on its private-sector debt.

Officialdom compounded the errors of piling debt onto borrowers that could not service their outstanding debts before the
so-called bailouts by making their holdings senior to private
investments, and by invoking collective action clauses (CAC) to
force private holders to accept the revised terms. The authorities
have partly realised the error of their ways. The ECB proposed
that its future purchases of sovereign debt would rank equally
with private-sector creditors in the event of a restructuring and
agreed to give up profits on Greek bond holdings to expedite the
second bailout. The coercion of the CAC turned the Greek bond
exchange into a default – the first of many unless the peripheral
states exit the euro. Even so, Greeks distrust (understandably)
their own government, so have shown great antipathy to exiting
the euro, and no other peripheral state has shown any desire to
leave.

Insolvency will keep dragging the euro-zone economy down
until both sovereign and bank balance sheets are repaired. Total
industrial production in the OECD remains below the pre-Great
Recession peak and widespread falling real incomes show that the
lower income brackets are in a depression. Other developed countries are in less dire straits than the euro zone, but slow economic
growth and deteriorating sovereign balance sheets are pushing
many of them in the same direction. Chapter 5 will discuss why
eliminating the European Ponzi debt without global contagion is

impossible and will offer some ways of minimising the damage and preventing recurrences – but deleverage is absolutely essential to restore optimum growth.

Unwillingness to leave a badly flawed scheme combined with unwillingness to create a federal union that could eliminate the current-account imbalances indicate that the euro is likely to implode. Implosion sounds drastic, but it may be the best outcome, because the required currency realignments would be effected quickly. This would avoid the runs on banks that would accompany serial exits and also amply demonstrate the need for structural reform. This does not guarantee implementation of the necessary reforms, but it does make them practical, which is a major step forward.

Banking problems are becoming more acute and Europe is the canary in the coal mine. The ECB barely offset the loss of broad money from loan liquidation – even though it increased its balance sheet by almost half in the last seven months of 2011. The same is likely to happen in other developed countries. This chapter has explained the European problems in detail. The next chapter will explore banking problems in a global context.

5

Too big to fail –
too haughty to learn

Small banks going bust has become a routine experience in the US, as 51 of them failed in 2012 compared with 92 in 2011. By contrast, governments fear that the failure of any large bank, regardless of its business model, would cause substantial collateral damage to the economy. Not only does the expectation that the government will always step in to rescue too-big-to-fail (TBTF) banks lower their cost of funding and raise their profits, but it also allows them to pocket the gains from their profitable investments while saddling taxpayers with the losses from their unprofitable ones.

Democratic capitalism gives individuals the right to the profits of their successful investments, but at the cost of bearing the losses of their unprofitable ones. TBTF violates this quid pro quo, so it is undermining the capitalist system and, by extension, creating immense moral hazard and jeopardising democracy itself. Unsurprisingly, executives of financial institutions that believe they are TBTF have exploited their ability to pocket profits and saddle the public with their losses, which include exorbitant bonuses based on ephemeral short-term profits. Government-mandated mergers and acquisitions during and after the 2008 banking crisis have greatly increased the size of TBTF banks.

TBTF is a perfect tool for the elite to exploit the public, and bankers are using their incredibly wealthy and powerful lobby to do just that. This long-running black comedy features the banking lobby bullying (read blackmailing) governments into sidelining public demands for bank reform, especially of TBTF banks, thereby penalising savers with negative real interest rates to keep propping them up, penalising borrowers with shrinking loans and, worst of all, greatly increasing systemic risk. The European sovereign debt/banking crisis will cause the failure of TBTF banks and the great danger is that one or more will prove to be too big to bail out.

Governments must limit the size of banks, increase their ability to absorb losses and be able to wind them down with limited damage to the wider economy when they get into difficulty – and there will always be a when. Banking crises have existed since fractional banks were invented in the 15th century and will continue until fractional banks cease to exist.

As it is, the major banks are reincarnating the absolute monarchies of a bygone era by considering only their own well-being – and the public be damned. Their intransigency is a declaration of their right to exploit the public (see below). The sole purpose of central bank (read public) funding for banks is to help them fund the output of goods and services. Instead, TBTF is transferring public money to fund losses from investment banking, insurance and speculation in securities, currencies and derivatives. By contrast, the public believes its money should not be used for any of these activities. In short, banks have declared war against the public and the public is definitely not amused.

Fraudulent activity surges in the Ponzi stage of the Minsky cycle, such as the scandal of banks rigging the interest rate underlying most transactions in financial markets, LIBOR (London interbank offered rate). The conviction of three Wall Street traders for municipal bid rigging has exposed a welter of unethical and illegal activities that have plagued financial markets for years. In a survey of 500 senior executives in the US and the UK, 24% said they believed financial services may need to engage in unethical or illegal conduct to be successful.[4] The desire to exploit all potentially profitable opportunities, taken to the extreme, ultimately involves defrauding investors.

Governments and central banks should be acting in the public interest, but their actions underlie the bad behaviour of banks. Chapter 2 showed that governments and banks have quintupled their share of GDP, and Chapters 3 and 4 showed that central banks printing money was the factor that enabled that cancerous growth. The consequent challenge of employing the ever-increasing amounts of excess liquidity in financial markets in the context of ever-diminishing creditworthiness spawned rising bankruptcies and ever more dodgy financial practices to avoid default. After the collapse of a primary dealer, Salomon Brothers, in 1991, the Fed ended its supervision and regulation of primary dealers. This highly criticised decision has led to a predictably rapid rise in dodgy financial practices in major institutions.

The New York Fed trading desk implements monetary policy through transactions with Fed-appointed primary dealers, making them the most important financial institutions in the country. Between 2008 and 2011, five primary dealers – Bear Stearns, Countrywide Securities, Lehman Brothers, Merrill Lynch Securities and MF Global – either collapsed or were rescued, showing that the ridiculously complicated US supervisory/regulatory systems are ineffective. The US has several, creating confusion and leaving many financial transactions unsupervised and unregulated. Major financial holding companies can select the supervisor/regulator they want. For example, the five major investment banks all selected the Securities and Exchange Commission (SEC), and there is a significant interchange of staff between investment banks and the SEC. No wonder the SEC and some other regulatory agencies have been so slow to act.

Furthermore, the unexpectedly large effects of the Lehman Brothers bankruptcy panicked governments into assuming the huge liabilities of failing and near-failing banks in 2008–09. Fearing contagion from any loss, European policymakers have tried to avoid imposing losses on investors where possible. Led by Ireland, European governments guaranteed all the unsecured bank bonds. These guarantees forced Ireland to nationalise all its banks and other European countries to nationalise or take major equity positions in one or more of their banks. The European Banking Association (EBA) threatened nationalisation for all institutions failing to meet its capital targets. As we will see later, so many European banks are TBTF that nationalising banks will be necessary to write off their bad debts and recapitalise them. This will cause significant losses.

TBTF banks are too big to exist. The only way to restore properly functioning capitalism is to break them up into pieces that are not systemically dangerous. The US Financial Services Modernisation Act of 1999 created TBTF by gutting the Glass-Steagall Act of 1933, which, in response to abuses similar to those committed by current TBTF institutions, had (rightly) prohibited:

• any institution from acting as any combination of an investment bank, a commercial bank and an insurance company; and

- any officer, director, or employee of a securities firm serving as an officer, director, or employee of any member bank.

Only the complete separation of commercial banking from investment banking and insurance activities can prevent retail deposit guarantees from extending to investment banking and insurance activities. Crying crocodile tears over bankers' bonuses solves nothing. Ending TBTF is essential to end the exploitation by the 1% of the 99%, but unfortunately the unbelievably big, powerful and wealthy banking lobbies have prevented significant progress in the battle to end TBTF. The basic problem is that banks have structured themselves so that the government retail deposit guarantee extends to all the activities in the non-retail part of the bank. This makes structural reform to remove the implicit government guarantee on the banks' non-retail activities difficult. Regulators have tried to restrict the growth of banks with capital and leverage ratios. Predictably, banks have found effective ways around both.

Other initiatives are also meeting major hurdles. The UK's attack on TBTF is to institute living wills, called recovery and resolution plans. Each bank will have to set out plans to return to health in the event of a fresh crisis and show how it will secure an orderly wind-up if the plans fail. The plans will have to be regularly updated and approved by the new Prudential Regulatory Authority. The Financial Services Authority has suggested that the plans should include emergency cash calls, the elimination of dividends, or putting the entire business of a bank up for sale. Bondholders will have to share in the pain. Bank structures will have to be simplified and clear knowledge of all counterparty exposures and how the banks' positions can be unwound is necessary to even begin constructing a living will.

The now much weaker than planned US Volcker rule, intended to prevent banks from trading on their own account while socialising losses with retail deposit guarantees, is a step towards separating retail and investment banking. Despite the massive JP Morgan Chase trading loss reigniting public interest in the Volcker rule, it was not finalised at the time of writing and will not go into effect until July 2014 – if the bank lobby cannot sideline it entirely.

The UK Independent Commission on Banking (ICB) is trying to go a step further by recommending ring-fencing retail banking from investment banking and wholesale funding, but stopped short of full separation. Under this structure, the UK banks' retail activities would take place in subsidiaries that are 'legally, economically and operationally separate'. Wholesale and investment banking activities would be outside the ring-fence, while banking services to large domestic non-financial companies could be in or out. The euro zone is proceeding with bank reform in the same vein, with the Liikanen review recommending the ring-fencing of banks' trading activities.

Nothing in the Dodd-Frank Wall Street and Consumer Protection Act deals directly with TBTF, but the ICB report does. As well as raising the equity capital requirement to 10% of assets and ring-fencing retail banking, it adds an additional 7–10% to the primary loss-absorbing capacity of banking institutions with so-called 'bail-in' bonds (regulators could write them down) and bonds that convert to capital under specified conditions (CoCo bonds).

Governments have been all too ready to put their hands in taxpayers' pockets before tackling the powerful lobby of professional investors. In July 2011, Bankia, a new Spanish bank collecting together various failed *caixas* (savings banks), was floated to a largely domestic audience, with 60% of the free-float going to retail investors. Less than a year later, the bank was nationalised and 2011 profits were restated from a €300 million profit to a €3 billion loss.[5]

Continental European banking authorities have ignored TBTF and did their utmost to socialise losses until the Greek debacle demoted investors who had paid senior credit prices for their bonds to subordinated creditor status. Worse, it threatened to make worthless the credit protection they bought in good faith. Who in their right mind would buy weak sovereign debt under those conditions? The first four years of the euro-zone crisis were completely wasted, starting with Greece's difficulties in 2009. In early 2013, Portugal is where Greece was a year ago and Italy where Portugal was a year ago, and Ireland lurks in the background. A default anywhere could have a domino effect.

Five more problems with banks

The imposition of Glass-Steagall-type separation of financial functions in a single institution will not solve five other problems. First, the 2008 financial crisis exposed a serious additional risk to banks with loans significantly in excess of their deposits. Wholesale funding covers much of the gap between loans and deposits. It can evaporate quickly, so the volume of loans in any institution accepting government-insured deposits should be limited to its deposit base.

Second, the investment bank cum insurance company remaining after the commercial bank has been separated may still be

TBTF. Higher funding costs and the imposition of higher capital and liquidity ratios on such institutions could help to limit their size, but history shows governments will rush in with taxpayer funding at the first sign of trouble. All major countries would have to pass laws mandating the separation of investment banks, commercial banks and insurance companies to keep systemically dangerous institutions from threatening capitalism again. Governments cannot avoid guaranteeing retail deposits, but they must prevent the cross-subsidisation of risky investment banking activities with safe retail funding.

Third, the current bank business model does not meet customer needs. An IBM study found a big difference between what banks think their customers want and what customers actually want. Big banks remain wedded to the one-stop-shop model of banking, hoping for the return of the days of soaring profits from opaque products (such as over-the-counter derivatives) that allowed inefficient pricing. This intransigence may end the era of big banks. Specialist banks more aligned with their customers' needs have seen their revenues and operating margins grow significantly faster than the universal banks.

As a result, IBM thinks the industry should split into three segments – to provide the infrastructure to facilitate capital allocation, relying on economies of scale to drive down costs; to give advice, such as wealth management firms and boutique mergers and acquisitions advisers; and to give superior investment performance, such as private equity and hedge funds – but few banks want to know.

Fourth, derivatives have created a synthetic banking system that is entirely separate from, but significantly affects, the real economy. The synthetic system manages cash flows equivalent to that of $707 trillion of real assets,[6] about 15 times the size of the global real money banking system, demoting the latter to a non-core activity at the major global banks. This enormous synthetic banking system overpowers the real system and imposes its pricing on the economy, thereby negating supply and demand in the price discovery process. Worse, it poses huge systemic risk to the real banking system because mistakes in the synthetic system cost real money. For example, mispricing structured finance and derivatives bankrupted Lehman Brothers and AIG.

Not only did these bankruptcies escalate a minor recession into the Great Recession, but they also caused systemic risk for the entire global banking system. In addition, the growth of speculation in commodity futures markets has priced commodities above their economic value much of the time. Producers and investment banks raked in fabulous profits from turning commodities into assets. Non-producers have paid the price for profiteering in commodities with slow global growth and declining per-head real incomes in many developed countries. The need to break up TBTF banks increases every day.

Fifth, some of the risk weightings the Basel Committee imposes to ensure banks hold capital commensurate with the credit risk inherent in their assets have been counterproductive. For example, governments that cannot print the currency they borrow in fail far more often than those that can. The UK's ability to print its own money spared the economy a much worse crisis in 2008–09. The zero risk weights on governments that can print the currency they borrow in have caused no problems. By contrast, the zero risk weights on peripheral euro-zone governments were a major cause of the European sovereign debt/banking crisis because they encouraged banks to load up on the debt of sovereigns that had previously periodically caused big losses on foreign holdings of their debt by devaluing their currencies and by default.

The 50% risk weight on gold has been equally counterproductive, as it prevented banks from owning the only asset not based on debt. Worse, banks' efforts to get around international and national regulations, some of them ill-advised, are effectively turning entire banking systems into one gigantic TBTF bank. The failure of a too-big-to-bail-out bank or sovereign will expose the lack of assets to collateralise the Ponzi debt created by government efforts to solve the problems of excessive debt by increasing borrowing.

European banks are too weak to survive a Ponzi scheme collapse. There is little doubt most euro-zone states would have to nationalise their banks in a further crisis and some of them lack the borrowing power to recapitalise them. Their ability to survive as independent countries without exiting the euro, devaluing and recapitalising their central banks in the devalued currency would be doubtful. Recovery on their euro liabilities would be minimal, causing the losses referred to above. Creditor countries and central banks would have to write off most of their credits to them, so the ECB and core state central banks would have to be recapitalised. Proliferating write-offs and bank recapitalisations would overwhelm the ECB and the European credit structure would collapse into deflation.

Chapter 7 will show that the Japanese prospered in their deflation because as a nation they are savers, not borrowers, and they invested their current-account surpluses wisely. Europeans as a whole are not savers and the current-account surplus nations did not invest their savings wisely, so Europeans would not prosper in their deflation. Moreover, all the funds to pay the costs of the soaring sovereign and supranational debt come from the private sector – ultimately households, as business depends on households for its revenues. With neither a strong balance sheet nor growing household incomes to fund recovery, the European deflation would spread.

Global contagion

The combination of public and private deleverage after the Great Recession has had a dire effect on household incomes, especially in the lower income brackets, in many developed countries. Greece, Portugal, Spain and Italy are mired in perpetual depression, incomes are falling in many other developed countries, such as the UK, where 2011 was the sixth consecutive year in which real wages fell, and the US, where real disposable income per head (read living standards) fell by 6½% to $32,720 in the four years to May 2012. In addition, the US Congressional Budget Office said 45 million people received food stamps in 2011, 70% more than in 2007, and the number would continue to grow until 2014.

Falling incomes should put upward pressure on fiscal deficits until a too-big-to-bail-out default creates a tipping point that initiates the implosion of the bad debt that has been accumulating since the early 1970s. The tipping point could occur for three reasons:

- Refinancing the bad debt from the housing boom is likely to peak. The Fed's decision to support mortgage-backed securities in QE3 and the nascent recovery in US housing may offset the worst effects.

- Concurrent recessions in Europe and the US would accelerate private-sector defaults.
- Sovereign defaults would make commercial and central bank capital evaporate.

The result? Defaults multiply, money supplies shrink and risk asset prices fall, causing the debt deflation that would have been done and dusted by now without the grossly excessive monetary and fiscal stimulation governments have used to avoid it since 2008. Deflation and negative demographics should reduce consumption and investment in developed countries. Only major restructuring and the more rapid recovery of emerging countries described in the following chapters can prevent depression in peripheral European countries from spreading to many other developed countries. Unfortunately, strong denial of the need to reform government activity to adjust to the new reality of negative demographics, the rising costs of entitlements, monetary policy impotence and increasing global competition are keeping the necessary restructuring of governments and banks off the table.

US banks are much better capitalised than European banks and the Fed's stress tests were far more rigorous than the European tests. Even so, a bank would pass the Fed's test even though a note on its balance sheet indicated that marking its assets to market would have more than eliminated its equity. Clearly, US banks must work through the remaining legacy of bad debt from the sub-prime crisis. Their non-performing loans are falling but remain uncomfortably high. The Texas ratio (see Figure 11) is the ratio of non-performing loans to net tangible equity plus loan loss reserves – the total buffer banks have against loan losses. Non-performing loans were well over double the ratio of that buffer at the peak of

Figure 11   **Texas ratio: US commercial banks**
%

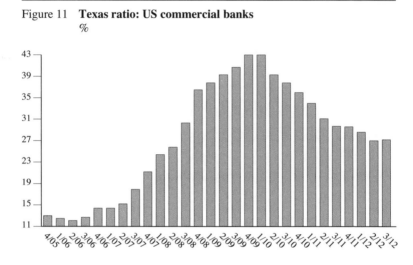

Source: Federal Deposit Insurance Corporation

the housing boom. Fiscal tightening in 2013 could negate support from the incipient housing recovery if unemployment rises.

Given the risks from both fiscal consolidation and euro-zone break-up, bank loan loss provisions at less than 60% of non-current loans (compared with 88% before the subprime crisis) look inadequate (see Figure 12). Non-current loans would have to continue falling to justify this level of provisioning, but a euro-zone break-up would pose major downside risks to this scenario. The banks can justify cutting their loan loss provisions, as the annual rate of net charge-offs fell from the 2010 peak rate of $190 billion to $87 billion in 2012. Loan loss reserve coverage has almost doubled to about two years of net charge-offs, but the big drop in loan loss provisions could prove short-sighted in the case of both a US recession and a euro-zone break-up.

Figure 12 **Loss allowance to non-current loans and leases**
%

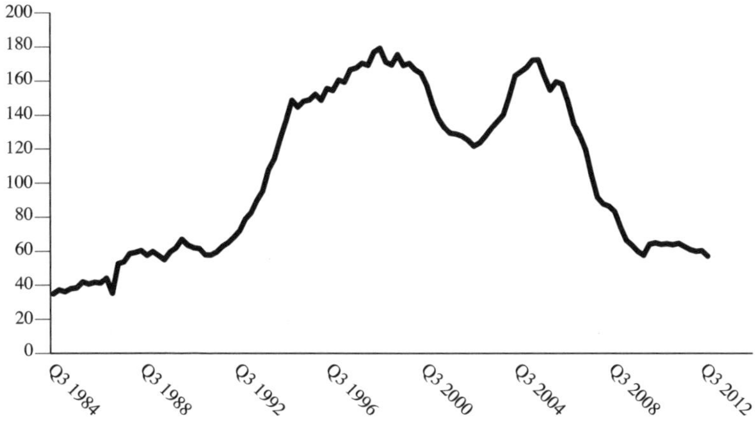

Source: Federal Deposit Insurance Corporation

Banks still have lots of assets with significant mark-to-market losses and the European sovereign debt/banking crisis could mean loan loss reserves would become grossly inadequate again. BIS data show that US banks' total claims on European peripheral state, German, French, and British banks comprise around 95% of US banks' total equity (see Figure 13). Banks' claims on government and the private sector are reasonably transparent in the UK but not in the US – leaving them exposed to a resurgence in concerns over euro-zone exposure.

US banks have become more profitable, yet are ill-placed to absorb increased loan loss provisions and the subsequent pressure on overall profitability, as 11% are still reporting negative quarterly net income. This is down from a peak of 35% in the fourth quarter of 2009, but above the average of 7.5% in 2005–06.

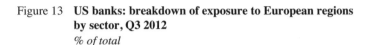

Figure 13   **US banks: breakdown of exposure to European regions by sector, Q3 2012**

% of total

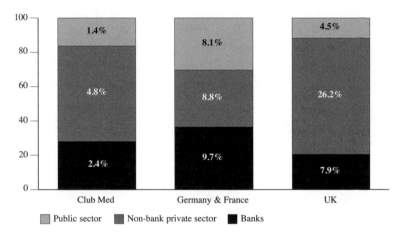

Sources: BIS Consolidated Banking Statistics; Federal Deposit Insurance Corporation

Net interest income was broadly flat in 2010–12, supported by modest private-sector credit growth and an ample supply of cheap deposits (see Figure 14).

Downward pressure on longer-term yields from slow growth, low inflation and Fed interventions should keep the recovery in net income growth subdued, even though large-scale creation of new deposits by the Fed should help to keep funding costs cheap. The Congressional Budget Office predicted that the legislated spending cuts and tax hikes would shift five percentage points of GDP to the Treasury starting on 1 January 2013 unless Congress acted. Congress reduced the five percentage points to about two. Unfortunately, the US economy is not strong enough to grow in the face of a shift of two percentage points of GDP to the Treasury, and a US slowdown had already begun in 2012.

Figure 14   **US banks: net interest income**
$ *million*

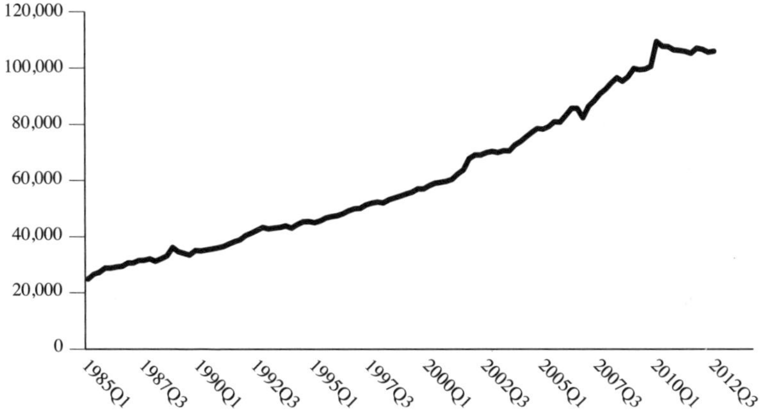

Source: Federal Deposit Insurance Corporation

A US recession may trigger a European sovereign debt/ banking crisis. Even though US banks appear to be well capitalised, with assets 11.9 times net tangible equity, they are in a poor position to withstand the double whammy of recession and a European banking crisis. They need an estimated $400 billion– 600 billion of capital to absorb the cost of marking their toxic assets to market, which raises their effective leverage to 19–28 times. Robert Reich of the University of California at Berkeley said that Wall Street's total exposure to the euro zone totals about $2.7 trillion. The double whammy is likely to cause problems for banks levered more than 13 times after marking all assets to market.

Excess debt is global

Global financial assets were only slightly greater than global GDP in 1980 but three-and-three-eighths times greater in 2010, with the increase in debt outstanding from a fraction of GDP to two-and-a-half times GDP accounting for most of the rise. Pervasive bad debt throughout the credit structure preventing many over-levered financial institutions from fulfilling their commitments caused the credit crisis in 2008. Only eliminating all the bad debt from the financial system (deleverage) can make it function properly again, which would drop debt outstanding and asset prices to levels that incomes and production could sustain.

Deleverage is anathema to governments and central banks, so they immediately began an all-out battle to prevent it. As a result, the People's Bank of China's balance sheet expanded by an average rate of 43% a year between 2007 and 2012, the Fed's by about one-third, the Bank of England's by over one-fifth and the ECB's by one-sixth. Printing money on this unheard-of scale reversed a significant part of the 2008–09 losses in asset markets – but the cost has been rising insolvency, particularly in governments and banks.

Rising insolvency is triggering record demands for liquidity. For example, demands for instant liquidity in the US have risen from less than 30% of GDP in the early 1980s to 70% in the early 2010s. That demand for reliable instant liquidity is helping to neuter monetary policy as $1 of the US monetary base now supports only $3.75 of M2, compared with almost $9 in 2008. Furthermore, US money velocity has fallen by a quarter since the mid-1990s, so $1 of M2 supports only $1.58 of GDP, down from $2.13. Clearly, monetary policy is a spent force. Deflationary forces are in control, not central banks.

As a result, Europe entered recession in mid-2012 and the US was slowing by the end of that year. Infrastructure investment is the best way for governments to combat recession, but it is not on any agenda and outsized deficits and soaring debt-to-GDP ratios would prevent implementing it if it were. Nevertheless, Mario Draghi's 'whatever it takes' bluff (see Chapter 4) raised investor confidence in financial markets to levels seldom seen in the last decade, despite the weak economies, fiscal problems, undercapitalised banks and weak leadership in developed countries. Belief that the US and emerging countries are leading Europe out of its misery is premature.

Most investors appear to doubt a European debt crisis would spread to a global one as the US subprime fiasco did. They are wrong – they should fear contagion for the following reasons:

- Most of the European problems noted in Chapter 4 are widespread.
- European banks are more highly levered than US banks were in 2008, so defaults should cause more disruption than the subprime crisis.
- Bank assets are a far higher ratio of GDP in Europe than in the US, so the banking crisis should damage real economies more and reduce world trade more.
- The US has loaned more to Europe than European banks loaned to US mortgages, even though Europe's ability to kick the crisis down the road is giving US financial institutions the chance to reduce their exposure.
- The Eurasian savings glut is turning into a savings drought.
- Seriously undercapitalised French banks, the main financiers of commodities trading houses, are reining in their lending, so trade lending, essential for global trade, will shrink considerably.

- Increasing production of shale oil and gas.

The Eurasian savings glut (see Chapter 2) was a big contributor to the massive accumulation of debt, but it is rapidly winding down. China contributed most to the savings glut, but its current account fell into deficit in the fourth quarter of 2011. It reverted to a small surplus thereafter, but China is opening up its capital account, so current-account deficits are more likely than surpluses in future. Japan was the next biggest contributor to the savings glut. Chapter 7 will show that Japan will continue to have current-account surpluses for the foreseeable future – but the ageing of the population indicates that the surpluses will probably diminish over time.

Rising oil prices increased the current-account surpluses of the oil-producing countries, but peaks in natural gas and oil prices occurred in 2005 and 2008 respectively and they are now considerably lower. Moreover, rapidly rising production of shale gas and oil will keep downward pressure on the prices of both. Meanwhile, the fiscal requirements of the producing countries are rising, so their current-account surpluses will fall. Northern Europe is in the worst position of all. Not only is its surplus with the struggling peripheral euro-zone states (a major part of the total) plummeting, but it will probably have to write off most of its accumulated credits with those countries. As a result, the Eurasian savings glut is over and the cost of equity capital is rising.

The enormous expansion of central bank balance sheets has hidden the rising cost of capital by enabling a significant fall in the interest rates in countries that investors consider to be safe havens – because bond markets are close to the money-printing process. As a result, the cyclically adjusted earnings yield on the

S&P 500 has more than doubled since 2000 while the yield on ten-year Treasuries has fallen by 75%. With forward price earnings ratios around 12, the average prospective return on equity capital is more than five times the average interest rates safe-haven governments have to pay. This yawning gap is stimulating speculation and hindering production by raising commodity prices (read costs) faster than incomes. This reduces the desire to produce and consume, and so is reversing the stimulative effect of printing money.

French banks are spreading the effects of this reversal across the globe. Their difficulties were a major contributor to the sharp contraction in global trade after the Lehman/AIG default, particularly in commodities. The quick restoration of bank liquidity explains the speed of the subsequent rise. The deep 'V' in trade caused an even deeper 'V' in commodity, energy and equity prices. French banks reining in their lending is at least partly responsible for the commodity indexes turning south again in 2011 before reaching the 2008 highs. Another banking crisis would cause a second sharp drop, but the insolvency of the French banks would not be so easily papered over this time – especially as investors have begun to link France with the peripheral states. As a result, continuing trade difficulties should be an instrument of contagion.

The credit bubble enabled longer-than-normal expansion phases in business cycles and shorter-than-normal contraction phases. The slow to non-existent deleverage that governments have engineered so far has shortened the expansion phases and lengthened the contraction phases. The inability to devalue threatens to turn the lengthened contractions into perpetual depressions in peripheral Europe. Developed countries outside the euro zone can devalue as its crisis spreads, but they are all in the same boat, so can devalue only against emerging countries – some of the biggest currency manipulators in the credit bubble. Currency wars threaten to slow growth further and the euro zone will be the biggest loser.

Currency manipulation increased inflation rates in emerging countries. Developed countries regained some competitiveness without deflation, but weakening global growth is reducing emerging market inflation. China is now grappling with deflation, so hopes that inflation in emerging countries would keep reducing the lack of competitiveness without deflation in developed countries is fading. As a result, conditions in the euro-zone periphery could easily spread to other developed countries – unless their post-devaluation policies differ radically from the euro zone's. Little indication of that difference has appeared as yet, so only a major banking crisis can save developed countries from protracted deflation or depression.

This chapter has detailed the problems in the developed country banking systems that would spread a European sovereign debt/banking crisis. The next chapter will describe the structural reforms that are needed and why they have not yet been implemented.

6

Absolutely necessary structural reforms

Reality cannot be ignored except at a price; and the longer the ignorance is persisted in, the higher and the more terrible becomes the price that must be paid.

Aldous Huxley

The financial systems and governments in Europe and North America need structural reform. Financial reform can be quicker and easier than government reform because the parameters for a properly functioning financial system have been known for a long time. Ignoring them was a major cause of the credit bubble and its collapse. As a result, the following five structural reforms must be implemented to create a sustainable financial system in developed countries:

1 The indiscriminate expansion of central bank balance sheets must end.
2 All TBTF companies must be broken up.
3 Banks accepting government-insured deposits must be prohibited from proprietary trading, investment banking and insurance activities.

4   All assets must be marked to market and the losses written off.

5   All financial institutions must be properly capitalised.

The indiscriminate expansion of central bank balance sheets must end

Chapter 4 showed that economies tend to function well over the long term when governments let market-set interest rates fluctuate around the natural interest rates. By contrast, inflation and credit bubbles abound when central banks hold interest rates below the natural rate. Various central banks targeted different measures of money growth in the 1960s and 1970s in an effort to control inflation and credit. None of them met their monetary targets consistently, so in the 1980s they began targeting inflation. Inflation targeting appeared successful in the beginning as inflation fell into the target zones. However, their definition of inflation omitted asset prices, and holding interest rates below the natural rates then produced the biggest credit bubble in history, which has now collapsed.

Inflation has not been a meaningful target for central banks because it only redefined the failed money supply growth targets, as both affect the same part of nominal GDP. In fact, the entire focus of central banks is wrong. A consensus developed in the post-war period that variable interest rates were undesirable as they would lead to greater volatility in output, so we ended up with interest rates fixed at too low a level and an enormous debt crisis.

Central bank manipulation of interest rates causes unnecessary economic problems by creating either inflation or bad debt. Chapter 8 will explain why, contrary to popular opinion, inflation is never a good thing. Here it suffices to say that central banks keeping monetary policy loose and expanding the money supply with quantitative easing has offset the disinflationary effects of bank deleveraging so far. The cost of all this freshly printed money has been a massive increase in the amount of bad debt that must be written off. Writing off the bad debts writes down asset prices by equivalent amounts. The only way to prevent both systemic inflation and the accumulation of bad debts is to restrict the rate of expansion of the central bank balance sheet to the rate of expansion in output.

Unrestricted movements in interest rates are by far the best real-time indicators of economic pressures. Central banks should be using them as economic barometers, not policy tools. The one policy tool that they can control completely at all times is the size of their balance sheets. As a result, the basic policy questions confronting central banks should not involve interest rates, but rather when and by how much to expand or contract their balance sheets. Central banks should moderate both sides of the business cycle by reducing their balance sheets in the upswings and increasing them in the downswings – keeping the net change in their balance sheets about the same as the change in real GDP. Restricting the growth of central bank balance sheets is the only way of keeping monetary growth under control through both business cycles and credit cycles.

All TBTF companies must be broken up

Chapter 5 discussed the necessity of breaking up TBTF banks. Even Sandy Weill, former CEO of Citigroup and the man responsible for dismantling Glass-Steagall, now thinks we should bring it back. However, the immense power and wealth of the banking lobby, its ability to corrupt officialdom and its ability to bury every administrative body in legal suits has blocked meaningful progress. As a result, the European sovereign debt/banking crisis will probably cause the failure of a TBTF bank that has grown too big to bail out. The sovereign debt crisis is already forcing banks in the euro zone to shrink their loans outstanding, and the carnage from the combined failures of the bank, the government and the central bank will not only push TBTF to the top of everyone's agenda, but also accelerate progress in all the other necessary bank reforms and, perhaps, even expedite the arrests of banksters for their malfeasance.

Banks must be prohibited from proprietary trading, investment banking and insurance

Chapter 5 discussed how TBTF banks pocketing the profits from speculating in stocks, bonds and derivatives, from investment banking and from insurance activities, yet using the government guarantees on retail deposits to force taxpayers to pay their losses, has eroded the capitalist system. The crisis has revealed the cost of deposit-takers-turned-mega-banks engaging in these activities. Losses at Merrill Lynch from underwriting the initial public offering of Facebook show that even core investment bank activities can be high-risk. The bank lobby may be slightly less effective in preventing reform in this area, but no significant measure is being enforced as yet.

All assets must be marked to market and the losses written off

Before the revaluation of gold in 1934, failing banks were wound down until their capital became adequate, merged with stronger banks or closed and liquidated. Then nationalising failing banks, writing off their losses and privatising them again became the common practice. The US and Europe criticised Japan for trying to keep its zombie banks afloat after its credit bubble burst in 1990 – then did exactly what Japan had done when their credit bubble burst in 2008.

Japan and the US recapitalised their banks, but neglected the crucial step of writing off all the losses. They appear well-capitalised, but hidden losses on their balance sheets cast serious doubt on their ability to withstand the European sovereign debt/banking crisis. Continuing refusal to implement this most basic technique for emerging from a banking crisis is a major stumbling block to bank reform and so to global growth.

However, as Chapter 4 showed, the European banking system is hopelessly overlevered and undercapitalised and its collapse should usher in deflation. The probable euro break-up should write off most or all of the euro liabilities owed by the peripheral states' national central banks and restore the power to print domestic currency and act as lenders of last resort to their domestic banking systems. The governments would then be able to borrow from their new central banks to recapitalise insolvent domestic banks.

All financial institutions must be properly capitalised

Banks face three types of risk: credit risk, market risk and liquidity risk. As described in Chapter 5, the Basel Committee risk-weighted capital regulations to ensure that banks hold adequate capital to absorb unforeseen credit losses must be revised to reflect actual credit risks.

Financial markets are volatile and market risk is the risk of an unforeseen drop in the prices of assets banks may want to sell.

Banks need adequate net tangible equity (total shareholder equity less intangible assets such as goodwill) to absorb the market losses incurred in bear markets. For example, Canada's regulation limiting each bank's total assets to 20 times its net tangible equity kept all Canadian banks out of trouble in the 2008–09 banking crisis. Few countries regulate the multiple of total assets to net tangible equity (leverage), and the 2008–09 banking crisis proved that limits are too high in some of those that do. Indeed, there is no guarantee that 20 times leverage would keep all banks out of trouble in the looming European banking crisis, but it would certainly help.

By contrast, all countries in the global payments system follow the Basel Committee's risk-weighted capital rules whereby all assets have risk weightings ranging from 0% to 100%. The required capital for each asset is the book value of the asset times its risk weighting. Banks meeting certain minimum conditions, disclosure requirements and approval from their national supervisor can use the internal ratings-based approach to calculate their risk weightings – i.e. approved banks can assign each asset and counterparty any risk weighting they want.

In practice, some banks risk weight up to 80%, and even more, of their balance sheets and the total of the risk weights of the other 20% can result in a net tangible equity of less than 2%. Net tangible equity is the only buffer against unexpected losses, so the bank's margin for error in valuation would be less than 2%. Indeed, potential losses due to the zero risk weighting of eurozone sovereign debt is the root cause of the European sovereign debt/banking crisis. The Basel Committee risk weighting has been supremely counterproductive.

There are two forms of liquidity risk. Chapter 4 showed banks, especially European banks, rely on wholesale funding which can disappear quickly. ECB and national central bank emergency liquidity assistance lending has covered lost wholesale funding for euro-zone banks, but some are running short of collateral. Moreover, all banks face the risk that normally very liquid assets become temporarily unsaleable. A primary function of central banks is to provide liquidity to banks with normally highly liquid, prime-quality collateral. Some central banks, especially those in peripheral euro-zone states, probably will not be able to perform this function seamlessly throughout a banking crisis, so a severe liquidity squeeze and significant unforeseen losses are probable. Banks would then need all the capital they can get.

Many banks, especially European banks, are unable to raise the equity they need in financial markets, but some are improving their capital by swapping bonds with short maturities for longer ones. This lets them both book a capital gain from buying back debt below par value and reduce the risk of being unable to roll them over when they mature. Converting debt into equity is a logical next step. The conversion should have a broad appeal to holders of subordinated debt in failing banks because recovery rates on the debt will be small while prospects for equity holdings in the same banks properly capitalised would be much better – especially as the claims of private holders of bank debentures are being eroded by both the senior claims of public entities and a flurry of covered bond issuance.

Even so, voluntary conversion may not always work. However, legislation forcing conversion of subordinated bank debentures (senior bank creditors are, mistakenly, completely protected by taxpayers) into an equivalent amount of equity as needed to maintain adequate net tangible equity would restore solvency to many banks. This would be an improvement on the totally unrealistic European effort to make taxpayers pay nearly all the costs of misguided investments in bank securities. Bondholders deserve no more than the receipt of face value in securities with growth potential in exchange for the eroding claims of their bonds. Unfortunately, banks converting holdings of debentures in other banks could create inappropriate, perhaps illegal, cross-shareholdings. Even so, netting out cross-holdings of bank securities would raise capital ratios by shrinking bank balance sheets.

Restructuring government

It is easy to see how financial institutions can be restructured to improve their robustness and efficiency, but much more difficult to say how governments should be organised. There is no clear-cut 'answer' to this question, with the argument deeply rooted in political philosophy, ethics and social values, as well as economic theory. Nonetheless, it is still possible to make fairly pragmatic recommendations on how the capitalist-based representative democracies most people in the developed world live under can better improve citizens' welfare without re-laying the foundations for economic and financial crisis.

This is the right time to be asking such questions of our governments. The backdrop which encouraged the expansion of government – strong global growth and easy borrowing conditions – has disappeared. Although there are grey areas in what the size and scope of government should be, current economic conditions are no longer conducive to governments spending large shares of GDP without making a productive contribution. Governments can no longer borrow large amounts from the future in the hope that growth will be robust enough to keep debt-to-GDP ratios in check.

A combination of ethical and economic arguments can determine the proper size and scope of government. At the heart of political ideas about what government ought and ought not to do there lies a tussle between equality and liberty – the further government moves towards trying to achieve equality of outcomes in, for example, healthcare and education, the more it impinges upon individual liberties. Various attempts have been made to resolve this issue, including John Stuart Mill's theory of utilitarianism (*On Liberty*) and John Rawls's 'veil of ignorance' (*A Theory of Justice*). Mill's guiding principle that decisions should be made to ensure the greatest happiest of the greatest number of individuals has become a keystone of modern economic theory, but it can lead to decisions which contravene common notions of fairness. Rawls's 'veil of ignorance' thought experiment asks individuals to imagine they know nothing of their position in society (the 'original position') and to choose what level of inequality they would introduce. This thought experiment leads to two principles of justice: one, that each person has equal rights to basic liberties, such as freedom of speech; and two, that inequalities can be introduced only if they allow the worst-off person in society to become better off.

These ethical arguments can inform more practical ideas on how and when government should intervene in society. The UK's Beveridge Report, published in 1942, identified five giant evils in society (squalor, ignorance, want, idleness, disease), which the new welfare state and the introduction of universal benefits were designed to eradicate.

Normative questions on the role of government are difficult, if not impossible, to answer, but economic theory can provide some guidance on where and when government should intervene to correct market failures. Government can help to provide public goods, funded through taxation, which the private sector would not otherwise provide because it is impossible to exclude free-riders. Government can also intrude to reduce the production of goods that have a negative effect on public welfare.

There are many ways in which governments can intervene. For example, a motorway can be funded through taxation or tolls; polluters can be taxed or cap-and-trade schemes can be intro-duced, as with the (failing) EU emissions trading scheme. These solutions are not always implemented effectively and they have different implications for the size of government. Moreover, even economic theory tells us that correcting only one market failure does not necessarily lead to an improved outcome – this is the theory of the second best, which we will return to in Chapter 11 when discussing derivatives markets. Government activity often balances the need to guarantee equality of outcome (such as in core healthcare services) and equality of opportunity (such as ensuring access to high-quality academic or vocational training), depending on individuals' capabilities.

Following a weak form of Rawls's second principle of justice, most governments wish to provide a social safety net but also the incentive to succeed and generate growth that benefits all members of society (introducing inequality to make the worst off better off). The extent of redistribution within the tax system is a balance of ethical and efficiency-based considerations. Most voters want to look after the least well-off or most vulnerable members of society and are happy to pay increased tax to achieve this – for moral reasons, to promote social cohesion and to insure against the possibility of falling on hard times themselves. The extent of redistribution needed in the tax system to achieve this depends on the level of services provided and efficiency considerations; marginal rates of tax set at too high levels can be a disincentive to work and so lead to reduced tax revenues overall.

Partly as a result of the 2008–09 financial crisis, but also partly through poor design and planning, many developed country welfare systems have unintentionally turned into Ponzi schemes, requiring increased entry into the labour force to fund payments for retiring workers. Few countries incorporate segregated investments into their public pension systems; the remainder are pay-as-you-go (current workers' contributions fund current pension payments). The IMF expects ageing to be the major contributor to public-sector spending on pensions over the next two decades, with expenditure expected to rise by 9% of GDP (in present value terms) over the next 20 years in the advanced economies – and by more if demographic assumptions prove too optimistic.[7] Indeed, poor demographics are one of the major headwinds to a healthy recovery, as discussed in Chapter 3. Contingent liabilities from underfunded private-sector schemes worsen the picture.

A combination of ethical, political and economic arguments can help to identify what kinds of activities government should undertake. But even if a consensus develops over, for example, whether government should provide universal healthcare, myriad questions remain over the extent and uniformity of provision, how consumers' preferences should be reflected, and whether the state should be both purchaser and supplier of goods. All these decisions have implications for the cost and size of government.

For example, completely private education provision is

certainly cheap for the state, but it is likely to leave at least some children without access to good-quality education (or to any education whatsoever). The state is also left with the problem of how to control quality, while lack of a generally good level of education in the population can lead to low productivity and a loss of economic competitiveness. This situation is unlikely to meet society's perceptions of fairness, but a 100% state system with a uniform curriculum may be perceived as unnecessarily restrictive of individual liberties.

Means testing of benefits is another thorny issue, especially in the UK, where government financial pressures are leading to a gradual erosion of the principle of universal benefit provision enshrined in the early welfare state. Withdrawing child benefit and, potentially, pensioners' benefits, from wealthier individuals is a contentious way of shrinking entitlements. Means testing can also create high marginal rates of tax for those moving off benefits and into work, discouraging re-entry into the labour force.

It is evident that governments are failing to deliver the kind of social benefits that voters would like to receive in an efficient way. Taxes are going up while government services and benefits are deteriorating. This is partly driven by circumstances beyond governments' control, such as increased globalisation of production and competition from cheaper foreign labour, but policy mistakes have also contributed. Not only has government become too big and increasingly inefficient, but it is also affecting various sectors of society disproportionately – yet not one has taken the necessary steps to deal with these problems.

For example, US Census Bureau figures show real median incomes have fallen to levels last seen in 1996, by far the longest period in which real incomes have not risen since the Great

Depression. Males in full-time work are worst off, with real median incomes in 2010 3% below the 1973 level. The drop in national real median incomes from the high in 1999 averaged 7%, but hit low income brackets much harder (–12% for the bottom 10%) than high ones (–1½% for the top 10%). The bigger hit to lower incomes has reversed the gains in lifting people out of poverty. Some 46.2 million people (15.1%) were living in poverty in 2010, the highest number since 1959 and the highest ratio since 1993.

The only way to prevent recurring major catastrophes, such as the Great Depression and the current depression in peripheral Europe, which a sovereign debt and banking crisis would spread to most developed countries, is to prevent sustainable expansions from accelerating into booms. Government is by far the biggest beneficiary of credit in excess of saving. This guarantees that government-controlled money will always be unsound money that ultimately ends in either hyperinflation or a credit bubble collapsing into deflation.

Fortunately, monstrous fiscal deficits and soaring debt-to-GDP ratios, tax hikes and cuts in government services and benefits are provoking considerable concern about the sustainable role of government and how to fund it. Some small, homogeneous countries have confronted this problem, restructuring and downsizing their governments with minimal discord. No large or diverse country has done so as yet and probably will not unless and until significant deterioration in the social mood – potentially after a euro collapse – forces it on them.

The era of indiscriminate growth in government spending is ending – unhappily. Protests against tax increases, difficulties in borrowing and external pressure from lending agencies and other governments have induced many governments to try to cut spending, but only those under severe pressure have done so. Their spending cuts have caused their economies to contract because the over-indebted private sectors have not been able to take up the slack the spending cuts created.

In short, the private sector and the public sector cannot delever together – yet they must. This conundrum is likely to cause a severe credit event. Predictions of the economic problems and the time required to emerge from a crisis are always too bearish and estimates regarding exiting the euro are no exception. Adverse circumstances concentrate minds on the pressing problems. Historically, economies have emerged from banking crises in 24 months, and there is no reason why the same should not be true of exiting the euro. Chapter 7 will show that economic revival does not pose a major problem. The big problem is that some countries may waste a perfectly good crisis by not restructuring their governments.

A severe credit event is inevitable

Bankers think they are in complete control. No meaningful bank reform will occur until an event shatters that illusion. Politicians and bureaucrats think they control their country's destiny – and, indeed, that of other countries. Euro-zone creditor countries are forcing the periphery to toe the line on austerity policies in the face of domestic violence and protests. No worthwhile reform of government will occur until an event shatters that illusion. Chapter 3 described today's unique conditions of both the absence of a balance sheet to fund the recovery of entities in trouble and the tailwinds in previous recoveries that have reversed into headwinds now. These adverse conditions should make the search for an easy way out fruitless. The long-delayed deleverage should collapse the tottering credit structure in a way resembling the monetary system collapse in 1931.

Citibank and Boston Consulting Group have estimated that $30 trillion of debt must be eliminated to get back to sustainable growth. The initial estimates of losses in crises are always far too low and the final figure will probably be double, maybe more. If so, asset prices should fall by about one-third. This extremely unpleasant experience is absolutely necessary for three reasons:

- None of the necessary structural reforms in financial institutions and government will occur until events overwhelm those who think they are in control.
- Economic growth will continue to fall until developed country government finances become sustainable.
- The credit structure is deteriorating rapidly and will continue to do so until all the bad debt is eliminated.

This chapter has explained the restructuring needed to solve today's problems and why it has not yet come about. We have now reached the end of the bad news. The next chapter begins the good news (yes, there is good news) by showing that emerging countries have often recovered from devaluation and/or default in as little as 24 months – because crises have a habit of focusing minds on solving the most important problems. This does not guarantee that developed countries can do the same, but it does offer a welcome alternative to years and years of trying to dig our way out of a major depression.

7

Lessons from the crisis-practised emerging markets

European peripheral states now face a similar style of financial crisis to that experienced by several major emerging markets over the past 20 years. These crises – Mexico in 1994, Brazil, Thailand and Russia in 1998, and Argentina in 2002 – were driven by fixed exchange-rate regimes leading to the accumulation of external liabilities by governments, corporations and banks, and culminated in financial meltdowns. European peripheral states have also assumed significant external liabilities as the corollary of large current-account deficits and government debt that would have to be negotiated into the domestic currency in the case of exit from the euro.

Currency unions are the same species as fixed exchange-rate regimes

The similarities between fixed exchange-rate regimes and currency unions have been all but forgotten in the European crisis. Many currency unions and fixed exchange-rate regimes have come and gone. A fixed exchange-rate regime involves one or more countries pegging their domestic currencies to the anchor currency; a currency union unites the domestic currencies into a single currency at about the same exchange rates as would have pertained in a fixed exchange-rate regime. Monetary policy maintains the peg in the fixed-rate regime, so the impossible trinity (see Chapter 1) demands capital controls for monetary policy independent of exchange-rate objectives, even though they are seldom 100% effective. The currency union's central bank sets interest rates for every country, so the individual countries have open capital accounts.

Under both a fixed exchange-rate regime and a currency union the market mechanism for pricing claims and obligations between participating countries is lost. By contrast, under a floating-rate regime, a country that persistently imports more than it exports experiences currency depreciation, decreasing the prices of domestic goods at home and abroad and raising the prices of imported goods, so rising exports and falling imports reduce the current-account deficit. A country that persistently exports more than it imports experiences the opposite effects: current-account surpluses and currency appreciation. These currency changes help to prevent the build-up of unsustainable imbalances between economies. Without this price mechanism, fixed-rate regimes and currency unions tend to develop big current-account imbalances.

Large current-account deficits cause inflows of foreign capital which will one day have to be paid back. As discussed in Chapter 4, persistent current-account imbalances are not a problem as long as the borrowed capital inflows are invested productively. If the inflows are wasted in unproductive investment, such as funding government deficits and/or cheap funding for banks to indulge in excess lending to the real-estate sector, significant vulnerabilities accumulate over time. Either the domestic private sector or foreigners must fund persistent government deficits. The location and funding of economic imbalances matter (see Chapter 8). An economy reliant on foreign capital inflows to fund the government deficit is in quite a different position to one where the government deficit is funded by domestic savings – which is the principal reason Japan's much-predicted fiscal crisis is yet to take place. Peripheral euro-zone economies reliant on 'foreign' capital (i.e. inflows from core states) to fund government deficits have found the opposite.

Furthermore, high domestic interest rates combined with a fixed exchange rate encourage domestic borrowers to take out loans in the foreign currency. An excess build-up of foreign-exchange-denominated debt in the private sector leaves private-sector and bank balance sheets highly exposed to a depreciation of the local currency. Once investors fear that loans might not be repaid, money flows out of the country, putting the local currency under pressure. Then speculation often causes devaluations, which, in turn cause defaults on the now much more expensive foreign loans. This is partly the story of the Asian financial crisis.

In the euro zone, all member states face the same nominal interest rate, but differential inflation rates mean real interest rates are different across countries. Where inflation is higher and real interest rates are lower, governments and the private sector take on more debt. The potential foreign-exchange exposure described above is hidden in currency unions. For the crisis economies, monetary policy interest rates and risk premiums both fell on entering the currency union. Rates were set by the ECB with a view to developments in the low-inflation core states. The assumption that no country could default within the euro reduced the perceived

Figure 15 **Average rate set by central bank, 1990s**
%

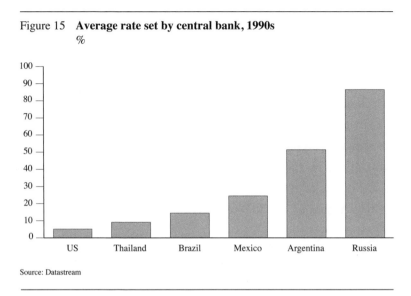

Source: Datastream

risk premium for peripheral state debt to absurdly low levels, causing a rapid build-up of private-sector and government debt to levels far beyond the capacity of the borrowers to service.

The ECB is slowing down the euro break-up

A currency union's currency floats against other currencies, insulating it from external shocks in the same way as it does for a single country. However, there is no mechanism for nominal adjustment between countries in the union, just as in a fixed-rate regime.

Euros tend to be recycled within the European currency union through Target-2. Euro-zone states need to devalue but lack the market mechanism to make it happen. Investors moving funds from Greece and Spain to Germany can put downward pressure on Bund yields, but put no pressure on national central banks. This merely increases Target-2 debits and credits. Thus nominal adjustment is not possible and all adjustment has to be real, resulting in deflationary pressures in the countries with overvalued currencies instead. By contrast, capital flight from a country in a fixed-rate regime can put intolerable downward pressure on the central bank's foreign-exchange reserves and result in devaluation. This financial market force on countries in fixed exchange-rate regimes will always defeat the finite supply of foreign-exchange reserves and/or the finite appetite of the central bank to raise interest rates to defend the currency and so avoid the need to deflate internally.

Foreign investors have shown some willingness to withdraw from the euro when crisis concerns are at their peak, but the currency has remained persistently strong. A higher policy rate and the recycling of capital flows within the currency union have played a large role in this. A resilient euro may reassure policymakers in core states that they are 'doing the right thing', but it also makes the challenge of real devaluation for the periphery even greater.

Life after devaluation

Greece restructured its debt twice but this has far from solved the problem. The debt write-down was far too small, leaving Greece with a debt burden of over 100% of GDP, in part because it left public-sector holders of Greek debt whole. ECB willingness to give up profits on its Greek bond holdings and lower interest rates on Greek debt are a drop in the ocean in the face of negative growth. Further write-downs will be needed – as will devaluation. Russia, too, carried out a 'voluntary' exchange of domestic GKO bonds for Eurobonds in July 2008, excluding bonds held by the central bank and state-owned Sberbank. The exchange bonds were priced at a spread of 9.4 percentage points over US Treasuries, compared with a spread of only 3.75 percentage points on similar bonds issued a year earlier.

This wide spread reflected market expectations of ruble devaluation against the dollar, which occurred just over a month later following heavy foreign-exchange reserve losses of around $1 billion a week. Market mechanisms brought about the post-restructuring devaluation quickly in Russia. The same forces are at work in Greece, but, without the ability to devalue, endless defaults and depression are inevitable without persistent fiscal subsidies from the rest of the euro zone.

The experience of countries coming off fixed exchange rates in the past need not make investors shudder. A currency crisis compresses a lot of the painful economic and financial adjustment into a short period of time with sometimes spectacular rebounds (see Figure 16). South Korea, Brazil, Mexico and Argentina saw real GDP declines of less than 10% after devaluation and/or default and GDP returned to its pre-crisis level within 24 months. Thailand's GDP fell 15% after devaluation and took five years to recover in real terms. Greek real GDP, by contrast, has contracted by more than 25% in less than five years with no sign of a turnaround.

The picture for equity market recoveries is far less encouraging (see Figure 17). For dollar investors in Thailand and Argentina, equity markets are yet to return to their pre-crisis peaks. The Russian equity market returned to its pre-crisis peak within two-and-a-half

Figure 16 **Nominal GDP, number of quarters to return to pre-crisis peak**
100 = pre-crisis peak

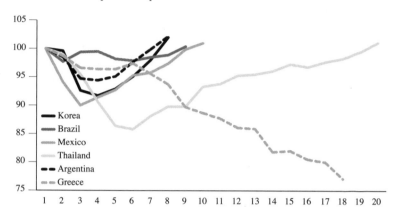

Sources: World Bank; Datastream

Figure 17 **Equity markets: number of months from pre-devaluation equity market peak**
100 = pre-crisis peak

Source: Datastream

years, however, and South Korea in just over four years (although it failed to hold these gains over the next five years). Brazilian equities took almost eight years to recover from devaluation and default. Although Russia was helped by rising commodity prices in its recovery, the absence of a banking crisis surely played a role in the speedy recovery – banks were vulnerable to devaluation because they held foreign-exchange-denominated liabilities, but were not exposed to a deteriorating domestic loan book.

Lessons not learned

The following seven lessons from past currency and financial crises have been ignored, contributing to the current crisis:

1 Fixed exchange-rate regimes and currency unions create current-account imbalances between countries in the regimes and unions.

2 Twin government and current-account deficits do matter.

3 The opportunity to borrow at significantly lower foreign interest rates encourages excess leverage.

4 The banking sector is a contingent liability of the government; what is bad for banks is often worse for the sovereign.

5 Defending an inappropriately set exchange-rate peg is costly and always fails.

6 Debt restructurings work with currency devaluation; without it governments are simply throwing good money after bad.

7 Large foreign-exchange reserves are not necessarily a sign of stability – they reflect the accumulation of foreign obligations in excess of the current-account deficit. As Robert Flood and Olivier Jeanne put it, 'reserves are expensive window dressing'.[8]

The early 2000s provided a crucial opportunity to fix some of the major problems of the global financial system, particularly in relation to banking oversight and how to deal with sovereign restructurings, but these opportunities were missed. The Asian financial crisis was partly driven by banks taking advantage of cheap dollar funding and extending unwise loans to real estate, highlighting the importance of good banking regulation.

A host of sovereign restructurings and defaults in the late 1990s and early 2001, including Russia, Indonesia, Ukraine, Argentina and several other Latin American countries, highlighted the reality that sovereigns do indeed default and a proper statutory mechanism would make the process less costly and more effective for both creditors and debtors. In dealing with crises in Asia, Latin America and Russia, experience clearly backs up the notion that, once a position of unsustainable debt has been reached, the best course of action is to restructure. Usually, an inappropriate and unsustainable exchange-rate regime is the first target. In this crisis, the IMF has instead chosen to prop up an unsustainable currency union, ignoring the lessons of the past two decades.

Around the turn of the century, some form of consensus had developed for the need for a sovereign debt restructuring mechanism. While statutory mechanisms can deal with corporations that become insolvent, no such mechanism exists for sovereigns. Of course, there are fundamental differences between companies and states. Companies can be dissolved, but sovereigns cannot. Company management can be replaced by creditors, but governments cannot. Nonetheless, some important principles from the management of corporate bankruptcies can be applied to sovereign states. These were outlined by Anne Krueger in a 2002 paper:[9]

- Allowing a majority of creditors (across all bond classes) to make decisions binding on all creditors, including the extent of forbearance and the terms of any restructuring.
- A stay on creditor enforcement in between agreeing a suspension of payments but before a restructuring is agreed.
- Protection of creditor interests as other policies are introduced, e.g. domestic bank restructuring and capital controls.
- Any new financing provided after the temporary stay on payments has priority over previous claims.

Collective action clauses were used in the March 2012 Greek debt restructuring to enforce participation in the private creditor debt swap, but CACs differ in a substantial sense from the first point – they apply only to specific bond classes and not to all creditors. A statutory mechanism, such as a new IMF treaty, would be needed to create the ability for a majority of creditors to make decisions during a restructuring. This kind of solution was on the table around ten years ago, but has never been included in the EU treaties. The US, however, does have Chapter 9 bankruptcy for municipalities.

The latest EU treaties (Nice 2001 and Lisbon 2007) were a missed opportunity to include a statutory sovereign debt restructuring mechanism for euro states. The case is often made that such a mechanism would increase the incentive to run up unwise debts as the cost of default is reduced, making default more likely. This may have been at the forefront of creditworthy governments' minds, such as Germany and the Netherlands. Balancing this are the benefits of reducing the final burden on creditors and debtors by addressing an unsustainable debt burden early on.

The Treaty of Nice, designed to modify the EU to allow

the entry of eastern European states, followed restructurings or defaults in Argentina, Ecuador, Côte d'Ivoire, Indonesia and Pakistan and was signed during a period of international debate over the merits of introducing a global agreement on restructuring sovereign debt. Even Maastricht was preceded by sovereign restructurings across central and eastern Europe and in Latin America. History had clearly shown that sovereign default is entirely possible and, indeed, current and future members had gone through that process themselves, including Greece, Germany, Austria, Italy and Spain.

8

Deflation is not a four-letter word

The classical definitions of inflation and deflation rates referred specifically to changes in money supplies, not prices. Central banks redefined inflation and deflation rates as the calculated average price changes in the prices of the output of goods and services, which gives governments and central banks four benefits. First, it diverts attention away from their continuous inflation of money supplies. Second, it lets them change the way of calculating inflation from time to time to lower the observed rate and further hide their war on savers with low interest rates and the growth in money supplies.

Third, it exempts asset prices from the definition of inflation. The public like rising asset prices, so central banks can print all the money they want as long as it flows mainly into raising asset prices. Indeed, printing money is the reason housing prices (read the cost of shelter) have risen faster than output costs. Rising shelter costs eroded living standards so much that, unlike the balance of history, one breadwinner per family has been insufficient for the past four decades.

Fourth, concentrating on output prices allows governments and central banks to be disingenuous when discussing the effects of inflation and deflation. They frequently point out that inflation favours debtors, asset markets and financial intermediaries, but never point out that deflation benefits savers and the productive part of the economy. Endlessly evoking images of the Great Depression has almost convinced consumers (who crowd into closing-down, end-of-season and Boxing Day sales) that low prices are bad.

By contrast, focusing on the vast majority (75% or more) of people who have enjoyed rising real incomes in periods of deflation would give an entirely different impression. Similarly, Western governments and central banks continuously harp on about Japan's 'lost decades'. Japanese financial institutions and speculators did lose heavily, but the general public became much better off as unemployment remained low relative to the rest of the world and the prices of everything from rent to golf course memberships fell and became affordable again. Western governments, central banks and bankers label deflation 'bad' and praise the virtues of a modest amount of inflation.

Even a little inflation is not a good thing

Treating the value of the currency and full employment as separate problems arose from a theory, originated in the 1920s,[10] that reducing inflation would raise unemployment and lowering unemployment would raise inflation, so monetary policy had to find the optimal trade-off between them. Belief in that trade-off created a widespread notion that a little inflation is a good thing, and its proponents use four main arguments to support their case:

1   The effect of overall price stability is uneven. Manufacturing prices have been falling, while services prices have been rising.

2   A little inflation enhances growth.

3   A little inflation facilitates the smooth operation of labour markets and so promotes maximum employment in the face of nominal wage rigidity.

4   A little inflation keeps nominal interest rates from falling too close to the zero bound, giving central banks enough room to cut rates should a recession appear imminent.

All four arguments are false. The first assumes falling prices hurt manufacturers, so central banks should aim for a little inflation to prevent manufacturing prices from falling. However, monetary policy can change only the overall level of prices; it cannot change relative prices. Productivity gains are bigger in the manufacturing sector than in services. Competition ensures those productivity gains will keep reducing the prices of manufactured goods relative to the prices of services, regardless of what central banks do.

As to the second, inflation does not enhance growth; it impedes it. From 1968 to 1983, US year-on-year inflation was never under 4% and average real GDP growth was well below potential at 2.5% a year. Inflation was over 4% in only eight months from 1991 to 2007, yet real GDP growth of 3.1% was closer to potential growth. Inflation lowers growth because tax is levied on nominal interest and capital gains income. Martin Feldstein and others have shown that reducing inflation to zero would yield big and permanent real income gains, as inflation-related tax distortions significantly reduce real economic performance.

Also, inflation makes it hard to distinguish relative price changes from movement in the aggregate price level. This ambiguity leads to errors in the assessment of prospective investment returns and so to the inefficient allocation of resources. Misallocation of resources lowers rates of real growth. Pessimistic price forecasts lead to underinvestment and overoptimistic forecasts lead to defaulted debts and restrictive credit conditions. A credible monetary policy of stable inflation would remove uncertainty about future inflation. That stable rate need not be zero, simply predictable. However, a steady positive inflation rate is harder to maintain than a steady zero rate because political pressure to lower interest rates to generate real economic gains is so much stronger than political pressure to raise rates to protect the purchasing power of the currency.

The third argument for a little inflation is that rigidity in nominal wages would stop wages from adjusting to changes in the relative positions of particular firms, industries or occupations if inflation were zero. That is, inflation greases the wheels of labour-market adjustment by letting some wages fall relative to other prices or other wages. This argument has three flaws. First, real wages are flexible because the price system allocates resources by setting relative prices. With zero inflation, the nominal wage becomes the real wage, so nominal wage rigidity would not survive in a zero-inflation regime. Jobs appear and disappear, and people move into and out of them so fast that the reallocation of labour dwarfs employment growth. Competitive forces eliminate anything that interferes with relative price adjustment that is not mandated by law or culture, so few labour markets in developed countries suffer from any big inefficiency.

The second flaw is the assumption that only cutting the nominal wage or letting all other prices around it rise can adjust mispriced wages, but two other mechanisms exist. Average real compensation rises as overall productivity rises, and real compensation tends to increase with seniority. Individual workers typically receive increasing real wages through time, so nominal wages may not need to fall with zero inflation, even in declining occupations. Advancing or delaying wage change relative to an individual's upward-sloping real wage path can accomplish the adjustments that inflation enables.

The third flaw in the grease-the-wheels argument is the fact that inflation puts more sand in the wheels than grease. A Cleveland Fed study showed that managements decide on the overall size of their wage pools, based in part on the expected rate of inflation, and then adjust individual wages and salaries in accordance with those budget constraints.[11] Sand results from poor inflation forecasts in the first stage causing suboptimal wage and salary increases. A firm may wish to attract high-quality applicants and fail to do so because the general level of wages rose faster than forecast. Also, workers' reactions to their pay raises often increase this sand effect by leading job seekers to incorrectly accept or reject offers because their estimates of inflation during the contract period turn out to be wrong. The study estimated the grease and sand effects separately. The grease effect was statistically indistinguishable from zero, even for low inflation rates, while the sand effect rose rapidly with the inflation rate.

The 'zero bound' argument for a little inflation assumes a much more constant economic response to interest-rate changes throughout the range of interest rates than actually exists. Figure 18 shows that nominal three-month Treasury bill rates have generally followed the inflation rate for most of the past 40 years. The zero bound view assumes that the interest-rate factors in the computer models that have been derived from this history accurately estimate the effects of interest-rate changes in the context

Figure 18   **US consumer-price inflation and three-month Treasury bill yields**
%

Sources: Bureau for Economic Analysis, Federal Reserve and Lombard Street Research

of zero inflation, i.e. those small changes in interest rates would have a limited impact on the economy. Experience proves they have as big or a bigger impact than large changes in the context of high inflation.

The economy responds far more to changes in the real component of nominal interest rates than to changes in the inflation component, so the economic impact of a given interest-rate change, measured in basis points, rises as inflation rates fall. So if inflation goes to zero and is expected to remain there, the inflation component of interest rates falls to zero and the nominal rate becomes the real interest rate. The gold standard era shows that the economic impacts of small basis-point rate changes were enough to maintain high growth rates with no inflation, even deflation. For example, wholesale prices fell about 2½% a year in the UK between 1870 and 1896 while output grew 4% a year.

The classic gold standard made zero long-term inflation credible and, from 1843 to 1914, British long bond yields ranged from a peak of 3.6% (in 1848) to a low of 2.4% (in 1895). Only small variations in long-term interest rates kept the economy on a non-inflationary track because the gold standard's automatic stabilisers allocated capital efficiently and limited credit creation, nipping both inflation and deflation in the bud. The Bank of England maintained this stability by adjusting the bank rate to keep the ratio of its gold reserves to its outstanding notes in a range consistent with non-inflationary growth.

Gold yields nothing, so the public desire to hold it depended on the rate of return on other assets. Higher interest rates raised the opportunity cost of holding gold, so the public desire to hold it fell. Convertibility ensured that the unwanted gold went into the Bank of England's reserves, raising its liquidity ratio to the desired level. Similarly, lower real interest rates increased public desire to hold gold and so drained the bank's reserves to the desired level. This price stability did not eliminate business cycles, unemployment, or occasional financial distress – but it did minimise all three. Moreover, all three rose whenever countries went off the gold standard, so the correct inflation target is zero. Unfortunately, a huge amount of restructuring is required before governments will permit the elimination of inflation, and, even if they do, achieving zero average inflation over time has never been accomplished without the discipline that a monetary system based on precious metals can impose.

Chapter 6 showed that monetary targets were a fiasco and the much-ballyhooed inflation targeting was an abject failure that led to the biggest credit bubble in history. Every past fiat monetary system has ended with a worthless currency and many are predicting the same end for this one, but preceding chapters have shown that the more likely outcome is a credit collapse reminiscent of the collapse of the gold exchange standard in 1931. The options for avoiding the recurrent collapses in the credit structure or monetary system are to end the incestuous relationship between governments and their central banks or institute a modern version of the classic gold standard.

The classic gold standard was the most effective monetary system ever. Under it many financial transactions had a direct impact on bank reserves. The resulting changes in bank reserves caused interest-rate changes that initiated financial transactions that offset the movement in bank reserves. These automatic stabilisers raised interest rates enough to cut off booms before they accelerated into credit bubbles and lowered interest rates enough to stimulate slowdowns into recoveries before they accelerated into depressions. Unfortunately, instituting a renewed gold standard to protect future generations from even worse credit collapses than the one we are now mired in will require a longer and deeper deflation than Japan has experienced. Even so, Chapter 11 will show how to prevent the worst abuses of fiat money.

The myth of Japan's failure

The US and European elite have continually warned that their countries will suffer the same failure as Japan if they do not follow the right path (theirs). How hypocritical! Not only do they disagree greatly about what that path might be, but also Japanese citizens have done very well during the so-called lost decades

– a lot better than Americans by some of the most important measures. The Japanese lifestyle has become increasingly affluent since the financial crash and, in the fullness of time, this era may be viewed as an outstanding success story. By contrast, the Census Bureau reported that the median US household income fell to $49,445 in 2010, the lowest since 1996.[12]

Japanese housing prices and the Tokyo stock market have never returned to the ludicrous highs they briefly touched in the final stage of the boom, but the following facts and figures disprove the claims of Japan's inferior performance.

- Japan's average life expectancy at birth grew by 4.2 years between 1989 and 2009 to 83 years. The Japanese now live 4.8 years longer than Americans – not from a better diet, but from better healthcare.
- Japan was lagging in internet infrastructure in the mid-1990s, but a survey by Akamai Technologies showed that 38 of the 50 cities with the fastest internet service were in Japan compared with only 3 in the US.[13]
- Countries with strong currencies generally prosper relative to those with weak currencies. The yen has risen 83% against the dollar and 89% against sterling since the stock-market crash in 1990.
- Japan's unemployment rate is 4.2%, a little over half of that in the US.
- According to skyscraperpage.com, a website that tracks major buildings around the world, 81 high-rise buildings taller than 500 feet have been constructed in Tokyo since the 'lost decades' began compared with 64 in New York, 48 in Chicago and 7 in Los Angeles.[14]
- Japan's investment of its consistent current-account surpluses in productive facilities abroad has created a large net inflow of investment income.

- The Japanese enjoy one of the most equal income distribution patterns in the world.

This list is impressive, but the national accounts show that US GDP has grown faster than Japan's for many years. Differing population growth accounts for much of the difference. Adjusting to a per-head basis narrows the gap to a meagre half of 1% a year, but that is still not the whole story. US statisticians have been aggressive in using hedonic pricing (adjusting the actual price for perceived improvements and additional features) to calculate inflation, which, in the view of many experts, artificially boosts a country's apparent growth rate. John Williams of shadowstats. com estimates the US growth rate may have been overstated by as much as two percentage points a year in recent decades. Far from being a lost cause since 1990, in the statistics that affect people's lives, Japan has outperformed the US in its so-called lost decades – even if Williams has overestimated the hedonic pricing adjustment by 100%.

Instead of foundering, Japan has reinvented itself in response to the emergence of South Korea and China. It could not compete in sectors where labour costs were a decisive factor, so it moved up the technology ladder and now makes the leading-edge components that China and others need to make products. The conventional wisdom in the 1990s was that Japan would be a major loser and the US a major winner from China's rise, but the reverse has happened. By contrast to the US's huge trade deficit with China, Japan has increased its exports to China more than 14-fold since 1989 and Chinese–Japanese bilateral trade remains in broad balance.

Furthermore, Japanese companies have been locating

manufacturing facilities offshore for at least 25 years and are buying foreign assets at a record pace. Japan is a rich country with big shares of global markets from automobiles to endoscopes, and it holds ¥251 trillion ($3.2 trillion) more in foreign reserves and investment assets than other countries hold in Japanese investments, according to the Ministry of Finance. This is a bigger net capital surplus than any other country in the world. Japan's economic model has not failed, but has rather succeeded in achieving most of the objectives the country has pursued.[15]

This has not been obvious because Japanese manufacturers have graduated to making producers' goods: precision production equipment and advanced components and materials. They are invisible to consumers, but the modern world cannot exist without them. The producers' goods industry is highly skilled and capital-intensive and so perfectly suited to Japanese strengths. Nevertheless, Japan's achievement is impressive because its major competitors, Germany, South Korea and Taiwan, have hardly been standing still. The world has gone through a rapid technological revolution in the past two decades, yet Japan's trade surpluses increased up to its nuclear disaster.

Visitors notice that Japanese prosperity is qualitative as well as quantitative as soon as they land at one of Japan's extensively expanded and modernised airports. They see that the Japanese are better dressed than Americans and have the finest models of the latest cars. The Japanese are consistently among the world's earliest adopters of expensive new high-tech items, such as cellphones. Japan, an initial laggard in cellphones, leapfrogged the US in the late 1990s and has stayed ahead ever since. Moreover, Tokyo boasts 16 of the world's top-ranked restaurants, compared with ten in Paris, the runner-up according to the Michelin Guide.

Similarly, Japan as a whole leads France in the Michelin ratings. Electrical output probably is the best measure of consumer affluence and industrial activity. Japan's rate of increase in per-head electricity output was twice that of the US in the 1990s, and Japan continued to outperform into the 21st century.

Japan's financial meltdown has given it some advantages. For example, Japanese trade negotiators noticed a change in attitudes in foreign capitals after the stock market crashed in 1990. The previous envy of Japan and serious talk of protectionist measures switched to feeling sorry for the 'fallen giant', and Japanese trade negotiators have been appealing for sympathy ever since. This strategy seems to have been particularly effective in the US. Believing that you shouldn't kick a man when he is down, US officials have largely given up pressing for the opening of Japan's markets – even though Japan never remedied the great US trade complaints of the late 1980s concerning rice, financial services, cars and car components.

Japanese residents have fared much better under deflation than European and North American residents have under inflation. A nation that can summon the will to pull together can turn even the most unpromising circumstances to its advantage. Japan's constant upgrading of its infrastructure should be an inspiration because it often requires co-operation across a wide political front. Such co-operation has not been beyond the US political system in the past. The Hoover Dam, that iconic project of the Depression, required negotiations among seven states, but somehow it was built and it provided jobs for 16,000 people in the process.[16] Indeed, the US may have a better record than Japan for reinventing itself when necessary, but it is lagging Japan now.

The real Japanese story is virtually unknown in the West and predictions of a financial catastrophe have been rife for years. Western emphasis on spending has obscured the fact that saving is the real key to wealth in many countries. By contrast, Japan is a nation that saves and so has consistent current-account surpluses. Japanese reluctance to invest abroad enabled Japan to self-finance at minuscule interest rates, so its massive debt burden has remained manageable up to now. But its immense debt, recent trade deficits and apparently intractable fiscal deficits have spawned numerous predictions of Japanese current-account deficits, forcing Japan to pay global interest rates and thereby triggering a sovereign debt crisis similar to those in the euro-zone periphery.

By contrast, Lombard Street Research's Michael Taylor effectively argued that investment income from a huge and ever-growing stock of foreign assets plus a large corporate-sector financial surplus will keep the current account in surplus for a long time. He further argues that the well-known and widely broadcast need to reduce the fiscal deficit has been reducing private spending because both the public and companies are saving now in the expectation of higher taxes in the future. As a result, the fiscal contraction should have a positive effect on the economy, as it did in Sweden in the 1990s and elsewhere, rather than the negative effects now being observed in the uncompetitive and spendthrift European periphery.

China's slowdown could hurt Japan

Japan's restructuring focused on exporting to East Asia. It may have to change that focus as the era of China's investment- and export-led 10% trend growth is over. The global slowdown has greatly limited China's ability to grow by expanding exports. Slowing export growth and rapid import growth have reduced its current-account surpluses from a peak of about 10% of GDP to either side of zero. Domestic demand has failed to pick up the slack, so China's trend growth has fallen from 10% of GDP to about 5%.

Past efforts to spur output growth pushed investment up to 49% of GDP, far above the highest level any country ever attained before. The maximum sustainable level of investment with about 5% trend growth is about 35% of GDP, so China is faced with moving a minimum of 14% of GDP from investment to domestic consumption. Investment has a multiplier effect on output growth that consumption lacks, so that 14% of GDP shift will be a monumental task that may not go smoothly, especially with the change in government that occurred in late 2012. Fortunately, China usually takes a long-term perspective. The good news is that the outgoing government, unlike the euro-zone elite, has made structural changes to bring about the desired outcome.

China's long-term goals seem to be to rise from a regional to a world power on the way to global hegemony. Before it can become a world power, the yuan must become an internationally traded currency; and before it can achieve global hegemony, the yuan must become the reserve currency. China must open its capital account before any of that can happen. No country with an open capital account can control both its interest rates and its exchange rate – the impossible trinity (see Chapter 1).

China has been controlling both, so opening the capital account is forcing it to relinquish control of either interest rates or the exchange rate. In fact, it is tentatively easing controls on both. Modest liberalisation of loan and deposit rates is in progress, even though the massive, bureaucratic and unprofitable state-owned enterprises depend on low interest rates to stay afloat. China also claims that the yuan is fairly priced and appears to be letting it float – but it would probably tame an undesired appreciation.

The People's Bank of China kept interest rates far below the growth rate of output (now called financial repression) while it effectively printed money to buy vast amounts of US and European securities. These purchases gave US and European buyers the funds they needed to buy Chinese exports (see Chapter 4). Meanwhile, the Chinese are big savers, and banks hold most of their savings. As a result, the low interest rates on deposits, often below the inflation rate, transferred a big share of GDP from households to the government and state-owned enterprises, so the share of GDP going into domestic incomes and consumption fell consistently.

In addition, low real lending rates created a real-estate bubble. Investment in real estate rose from 2.4% of GDP before the financial repression 'tax' started to 9.1% in the first half of 2011. Official claims that rising migration to cities was causing the huge increases in real-estate investment were rubbish. Migration to cities fell from 24 million to 19 million a year over the period, leaving many newly built cities and shopping malls almost vacant. The financial repression funded other investments, many of which, like real estate, were wasted, so debt increased faster than the ability to service it and the rising debt burdens are slowing investment. The steel and shipbuilding industries have been hit especially hard. China is in a later stage of the Minsky credit cycle than most other emerging countries. This will be discussed further in Chapter 11.

Lombard Street Research calculations show output growth fell below the 5% trend growth rate in 2012 and investment should keep falling. By contrast, household income growth remained at about 10%, so domestic consumption should be picking up some of the slack. The government cut interest rates and lowered banks' required cash reserve ratios. This is not more financial repression because China is opening the capital account, albeit covertly, thus offsetting the repression. As a result, interest rates are falling more slowly than inflation. In addition, slower growth is unlikely to derail either the following market reforms or the effort to increase reliance on consumption for growth.

The efficiency of government depends much more on the quality of leadership than on the fairness of its selection. The dismissal of Bo Xilai, a representative of the hard left, may have been necessary to continue the programme of substantial market reform, which includes:

- establishing an electronic market to provide another platform to fund small business;
- establishing the China International Payments system – comparable to SWIFT;
- easing capital transfers in and out of China;
- establishing foreign markets for yuan-denominated debt;
- broadening the permitted trading range of the yuan;
- extending China's network of international swap agreements.

The first two will improve internal market functions, but the last four should transform the Chinese economy and its interaction in global affairs. Easing capital transfers into and out of China has begun to open the capital account. Far-below-market interest rates require a closed capital account, so opening it, together with the slowing GDP and investment growth, is easing financial repression and household incomes and consumption should continue to grow faster than GDP. Incomes may not slow much from their current 10% growth rates if markets are allowed to work – a big ask from a government accustomed to universal control, especially one involved in a changing of the guard. However, the authorities have set up a viable plan to implement their promise to increase reliance on domestic consumption for growth.

Opening the capital account is allowing an outflow of money from China. Many wealthy Chinese have applied for emigration permits and are exporting their capital. Canada is one of the popular destinations, along with Singapore and the US. Incoming Chinese money created bubbles in the Vancouver and Toronto real-estate markets with actual house prices peaking at about 11 and 9 times incomes respectively, although official figures show somewhat lower levels. Other capital exports are less obvious, but, along with the current account on either side of zero in 2012, they have been enough to slow the upward drift of the yuan and foreign-exchange holdings. The broadening of the trading range was probably intended to enable yuan depreciation and foreign sales of yuan-denominated debt to cover domestic capital exports and current-account deficits.

Chinese banks are a big problem. Fast growth minimised their bad debt problems in the past and banks have paid outsized dividends. The big four banks paid 144 billion yuan in dividends and raised 200 billion yuan on capital markets in 2011. Slowing growth will increase losses and diminish revenues, so they will need much larger recapitalisations in the future. Like financial repression, bank recapitalisations diminish household incomes and consumption. This will complicate the transfer of GDP from investment to consumption. The Chinese economy appears to be recovering and the transition from investment to consumption seems to be progressing relatively smoothly. Even so, all the risks are on the downside in such a big move, especially with the need for bank recapitalisation.

Japan invested its current-account deficits in productive facilities abroad and the income from them is funding a large government-sector deficit. By contrast, China had invested most of its current-account surpluses in interest-bearing paper at relatively low interest rates, but this policy is changing. China's overinvestment and the structural adjustment of raising consumption at the expense of saving and investment have eliminated the current-account surpluses. By contrast, the gradual opening of the current account will allow Chinese domestic savings to find more productive growth opportunities abroad, such as natural resources and infrastructure investment in Africa. As a result, an increasing flow of foreign earnings will soon begin to assist the Chinese transition, just as it did for the Japanese one.

According to Diana Choyleva of Lombard Street Research, rapidly rising Chinese labour costs relative to the US mean that the dollar–yuan exchange rate is now at about fair value. This means that China's massive vendor financing scheme described in Chapter 4 has ended. The resulting accumulation of Chinese foreign-exchange reserves was a big part of the Eurasian savings glut, much of which flowed into dollars – 25% of US Treasuries are currently held on the Chinese mainland. The end of China's current-account surpluses has ended its Treasury purchases and capital outflows will cause Chinese sales of Treasuries. Furthermore, the growth of international foreign-exchange reserves has slowed sharply. Americans will have to buy far more Treasuries in the future, so US interest rates should rise in spite of deflation.

This chapter has shown that deflation, far from being the monster Western governments and central banks have portrayed, is beneficial to nations that save. Unfortunately for Japan and the West, China will not be the global locomotive people are hoping for, but its trend growth rate of 5% will help Europe and North America to return to optimal growth – after they have made the necessary structural reforms. The next few chapters will show that other emerging countries will also help developed countries emerge from the European sovereign debt/banking crisis.

9

An end to the euro

Several currency unions that were not political have come and gone. The euro is notably the most unsuitable agglomeration of countries ever to be bundled together in a currency union. It includes hard-currency countries that abhor inflation, soft-currency ones that routinely inflate their way out of debt problems, countries that do not know which they are, and one that was in default for half its existence as an independent country before joining the euro. Expecting that they would all become hard-currency countries overnight was ridiculous and astute observers noted the euro was doomed before it was launched.

Central bank hype has induced financial markets to expect miracles from them, but their hype has all the substance and none of the pizzazz of the Wizard of Oz. Chapter 6 showed that the ECB could not prevent the Greek default and, in its current form, cannot prevent any future sovereign default. Furthermore, its lack of a backstop to bail it out of negative equity limits its lender-of-last-resort capabilities for banks to its capital and reserves. They total about €500 billion, before marking its assets to market. The ECB has levied big haircuts on dubious collateral, but its interference in financial markets has made it hard to determine realistic prices for peripheral state liabilities in the absence of that interference. Also, potential losses in future crises are always underestimated, so it is safe to say that the actual deployable equity and reserves are less than the book value.

The book value of current ECB assets is a conservative 6.2 times equity and reserves and it should be, as Greece has proven that the recovery on some peripheral state liabilities will end up being close to zero. That leverage rises to a much less comfortable 9 times if we assume that current mark-to-market losses total 5%. The ECB is careful not to release data that would enable an educated guess about that number, so 5% may be a significant underestimate and the leverage would then be well over 9 times. The mark-to-market losses on the assets presently held will rise as the crisis progresses, and the losses on the assets acquired in the future will be higher. Sticking with the 9 times leverage, and assuming the ECB's limit is 13 times (7.7% losses on assets would wipe out capital and reserves), would enable the ECB to expand its balance sheet by €1.4 trillion.

Obviously, these figures are highly subjective and other analysts would derive different ones. Moreover, banks and central banks have operated with negative equity before and some have returned to health by winding down their balance sheets; but a central bank winding down its balance sheet is particularly unhelpful in a crisis. The 27 member states could recapitalise the ECB in that eventuality, but the glacial speed of European operations means that completing the process before the damage owing to the lack of a lender of last resort had already been wrought would be unlikely. There would be little sense of urgency as the ECB certainly has the capability of facilitating peripheral state exits from the euro.

The failure of the €1 trillion long-term repurchase operation in December 2011 and February 2012 to repair bank balance sheets enough to permit loan expansion shows that ECB lending capacity of €1.4 trillion is a drop in the ocean compared with the combined requirements of the peripheral states. According to Elliot Wave International, Europe has spent 'an unprecedented $3 trillion-plus in bailouts, monetary transfusions, AND [emphasis in original] toxic debt transplants' so far.[17] That $3 trillion includes the $1.2 trillion that European banks have parked at their national central banks (NCBs) and the Target-2 credits, such as the Bundesbank's net credit, which then was €615 billion (23% of German GDP). Technically, the money was lent, not spent, but the euro value recovered on most peripheral European liabilities in a crisis could be small.

Mario Draghi bluffed (see Chapter 4) because the ECB does not have the ammunition to prevent contagion in the rest of Europe. Portugal, Spain, Italy and some smaller countries have precisely the same competitiveness problems as Greece and an exit, far from clearing the air, would put increasing pressure on their finances. Bank runs in peripheral states would accelerate and the imbalance of debts and credits in the Target-2 system would soar, triggering the need to introduce capital controls to alleviate the runs on peripheral state banks.

The NCBs guarantee the deposits in their commercial banks and administer the emergency liquidity assistance (ELA) programme, which lends them money when they have liquidity problems. Peripheral state NCBs make the most ELA requests and accept the most dubious collateral. The implicit assumption that no NCB would ever default removed credit monitoring from the European Target-2 banking system. As a result, persistent payments imbalances (that in bank-to-bank transactions would have caused credit to be cut off) have created massive accumulations of liabilities that otherwise would never have been permitted.

The Greek default and yo-yoing yields on Spanish and Italian bonds prove that the $3 trillion lent to hold the euro together did nothing to improve solvency. Indeed, more loans can only buy time – and then only as long as people are willing to believe that the increasing debts can be rolled over forever. Worse, each euro of additional loans threatens, in most cases, to add a euro to the bad debt that ultimately must be written off. Most of the external liabilities of Greece, Portugal, Spain and Italy would have to be written off. European creditor countries and their banks own most of those liabilities, so the losses would eventually force the nationalisation of all euro-zone, and possibly all European, banks.

So far Europeans have generally made every effort to keep the bondholders of their banks whole at the expense of taxpayers – in part because some of the bondholders are also retail depositors. Retail deposits are a crucial part of the intermediation of saving, so protecting them is a legitimate function of government. By contrast, bank bonds are liability management tools to increase bank profits, so protecting bank bondholders is not a legitimate function of government. It places a needless burden on taxpayers and continuing this practice would be the best way to spread the depression in peripheral states to the rest of Europe.

Chapter 6 showed that converting debt to equity is the fairest and the most efficient way to recapitalise banks and that alone would be sufficient to return some banks to viability. Most countries will probably establish a 'bad bank' to dispose of the toxic assets of banks. The bad bank paying market prices for the assets would ensure that the commercial banks wrote off all their losses and would minimise the cost to taxpayers. However, it would also maximise the cost of recapitalisation. Core state governments probably have enough borrowing power to establish bad banks and to recapitalise the commercial banks. Peripheral states do not and the ECB cannot, as constituted, lend them the money to do so.

As a result, peripheral states are borrowing from the EFSF and ESM (see Chapter 4) to recapitalise their banks. This is futile for two reasons. First, they have not purged the toxic assets from bank balance sheets, so will have to keep recapitalising them. Second, the EFSF and ESM have a total lending authorisation of €500 billion and persistent calls to raise it have failed. Even if the authorisation were raised, it still would be woefully inadequate. The larger peripheral states will not be able to borrow enough to nationalise their banks and stay in the euro. The countries that cannot borrow enough to recapitalise their banks must exit the euro – so that they can borrow their depreciated national currency from their central banks to establish their bad banks and recapitalise their commercial banks – or sink into ever deeper depression. Increasing bank capital is the only transaction that immediately and permanently reduces the money supply by an equal amount. Printing money to recapitalise their banks would postpone its deflationary effects to the time the banks are privatised.

Recapitalised banks without deflation should give peripheral states an advantage over core states, some of which could use virtually all their borrowing power to recapitalise their banks and all of which probably will have great difficulty selling bank equity at reasonable prices in the aftermath of two banking crises in quick succession. Selling equity in a bank with a clean balance sheet at less than book value would increase the deflationary effects of the recapitalisation unless the purchasers are foreign residents.

An insightful Lombard Street Research special report by Charles Dumas, *The Netherlands & The Euro*, detailed the cost to the Netherlands of being in the euro and exiting. It showed that residents of countries that stayed out of the euro, such as Sweden and Switzerland, prospered greatly relative to core states in the euro, such as Germany and the Netherlands. It concluded that exiting the euro would be far cheaper than staying in and left the strong impression that the same would be true for other core states, especially Germany. Even so, few people believe that a core state will exit the euro, especially Germany, because its currency would be revalued upwards. They may be right, but politics, not economics, is controlling the European situation.

The German economic structure and demographics make it dependent on exports for growth. The euro zone is its biggest export market by far, so Germany needs it to prosper. The German drive to lower its costs has exploited the euro zone, and Germany must both underwrite peripheral state debt and create a credible path to more union. Meanwhile, the imposition of austerity is fuelling anti-German sentiment and euro-zone member states are drifting apart. The myth that peripheral states are taking advantage of Germany is wearing thin and companies are avoiding credit risk in Europe where possible. As a result, the chances of Germany accomplishing both these Herculean tasks in time to avoid the looming European sovereign debt/banking crisis are small, so the most likely scenario is that the euro zone will eventually break up.

Germany is trying hard to hold the euro together as any untoward event could quickly destroy the myth of the euro's invincibility. Investor confidence is hovering around multi-year highs and currently betting on German success, but real incomes are falling, banks are not lending and peripheral state collateral for borrowing at the ECB is becoming ever more suspect, so the required growth and/or inflation is highly unlikely.

An exit from the euro would greatly aggravate the bank runs, requiring capital controls as noted above, which seldom work well, and so would force other countries to exit the euro to fund the recapitalisation of their banks by printing their national currencies. Peripheral states exiting the euro would crystallise the losses inherent in their rapidly accumulating liabilities to creditor countries. The prospect of those losses, which would end up being far bigger than anyone expects, is reducing the credit ratings of core states and their decline would accelerate as the crisis progresses. The speed with which the euro unravels would be frightening – a fit ending to the folly of its construction.

Banks post-euro

Banks have often faced the problem of sudden devaluation or sovereign default, both of which put enormous pressure on capital and funding. Sovereign bonds and foreign-currency-denominated loans often make up a large portion of a bank's assets and both are subject to potential losses. A sharply depreciating currency raises the cost of a bank's foreign borrowing and makes it more expensive for it to roll over foreign-exchange swaps. The prospect of large capital losses for some banks makes it more difficult for all banks to secure funding in the interbank markets because no one knows where the losses will be.

There are two differences between past episodes and the current predicament. First, the euro would ultimately cease to exist except as a legacy currency following devaluation and default. Second, the ECB is already able to provide emergency liquidity to troubled banks in a way that a fixed exchange-rate regime central bank cannot. The Greek euro-zone farce is such a long-drawn-out process because banks are able to subsist on emergency ECB funding as deposits leak away.

For this reason, runs on banks as depositors try to escape forced conversion from euros to domestic currency are unlikely to be the trigger for break-up of the currency union. Troubled euro-zone sovereigns are likely to issue debt at shorter and shorter maturities. Ultimately, inability to roll over debt at manageable rates and no realistic prospect of reducing the stock of debt could provoke an exit from the euro, although the Draghi bluff has temporarily circumvented this risk. A decision by creditors not to disburse further funds could, therefore, be the final straw, as with the IMF's refusal to Argentina in December 2001. Default and/or exit is also more likely to occur when governments reach primary balance. With no need to access markets to fund day-to-day government spending, the incentive is greater to default on the existing debt stock. Once the break-up is in motion, some form of deposit freeze or capital controls seems unavoidable. The strong link between banks and their sovereign means recovery rates from defaults within the euro are likely to be small.

Argentina's approach to bank deposit outflows in the run-up to devaluation is a study in what not to do. Argentina had a history of confiscating deposits to finance the government, having done so in 1982 and 1989.[18] As pressure on the government finances intensified in 2001, there was a genuine fear that these actions would be repeated. To prevent large-scale deposit flight, deposits were frozen. Assets and liabilities were converted at an asymmetric rate, with dollar liabilities converted to pesos at a rate of $1 to Ps1.4, but dollar assets were converted at a one-to-one rate, creating a large gap between assets and liabilities on banks' balance sheets. Euro-zone devaluation will probably entail conversion of domestic assets and liabilities to the new currency at a one-to-one rate.

On leaving a fixed exchange-rate peg, a central bank can resume its role as lender of last resort, but only in the domestic currency. For outstanding foreign-exchange funding needs, external help is still required. Following the 1994 Mexican devaluation, the central bank provided $4 billion of liquidity at penalty rates to the domestic banks, drawing on resources from the US and IMF bailout package. Banamex was able to return to the markets in May 1995, and by September 1995 these loans had been repaid.[19]

Banks do not simply default on their external liabilities in case of sovereign default and devaluation. Devaluing countries will need to negotiate haircuts on any remaining euro liabilities. A short moratorium on external debt payments and margin calls is likely to take place, as in Russia in 1998. The ECB would continue to exist as a legacy central bank and, as euro liabilities are written down or paid off in new national currencies, the euro money supply would shrink away over time. If the ECB were to be wound up with negative net worth, the losses would be borne by former euro-zone states according to their proportion of ECB share capital.

The major difference between devaluations of the past and the euro-zone debacle is that euro-zone external liabilities are not denominated in dollars but in euros, a currency that would ultimately cease to exist. The Fed could act in concert with the

ECB to provide emergency euro and dollar swap facilities to new euro-zone national central banks to replace maturing funding, as part of co-ordinated IMF support to the region. The banks can repay these loans once access to wholesale markets is restored, albeit at a higher cost than before the crisis.

To address the excess stock of commercial bank debt extended to Latin American countries in the 1980s, commercial bank loans to sovereigns were swapped for new, discounted sovereign bonds, dubbed Brady bonds in honour of Nicholas Brady, the Treasury secretary who invented them. The issuing country used IMF or World Bank funding to buy zero-coupon US Treasuries to meet the principal at maturity. In this case, dollar debt was backstopped by dollar collateral. A similar approach could work for post-euro sovereign debt using gold as collateral.

Recapitalising the banks

Where more useful lessons can be learned from Argentina is in the methods used to recapitalise its banks. To fill the gap on banks' balance sheets created by pesofication, and in spite of the sovereign default, Argentina issued new debt. The domestic regulator allowed banks to hold these bonds on their balance sheets at face value. The yield was in the low single digits and inflation adjustments were capitalised over time.[20] In spite of forced pesofication and attempts to convert deposits to government bonds, by the time the deposit freeze ended in December 2002, deposits were already rising.

Argentina's banking system entered the currency and government debt crisis with high levels of equity capital, in excess of

20% of risk-weighted assets, and clever financial manoeuvring by the authorities averted a major solvency crisis following default. The combined impact of conversion from dollars to pesos, devaluation and the transfer of new government bonds to the banks meant that total public-sector assets held by the banking system increased by over 80% between December 2001 and January 2002. Capital rose by almost 30%. With equity at scarce levels in the euro zone, Argentina's chosen route to shoring up the banking system is unlikely to be an option, although it does highlight investors' tolerance to new sovereign liabilities issued post-default. Transferring bonds to banks at face value (preferably temporarily) means any interest received can help to restore profitability, depending on the ability of the sovereign to pay. The bonds can then be used as collateral to obtain funding in the open markets (if they are functioning).

Russian banks also had substantial exposure to the public sector at the time of government default, but the authorities took a different approach to their solvency issues. Claims on the government made up over 30% of total assets in the run-up to the 1998 crisis. As pressures in the bond market mounted, the banks faced increasing margin calls as the value of sovereign collateral declined. Liquidity pressures arose as depositors switched out of roubles and into dollars and the cost of rolling over dollar funding increased. The central bank had to step in and provide a $100 million loan to SBS-Agro as it was overwhelmed by margin calls on dollar-denominated government debt.[21] This loan was reportedly collateralised by 75% of the bank's equity, although the company denied this.[22] Following the sovereign default, an IMF review found 15 out of the 18 largest banks had negative net worth, with 28% of capital wiped out through exchange-rate losses, 13% from government debt losses and 34% from loan-loss provisions.[23]

Mexico followed a similar route to Russia following its 1994 devaluation. To recapitalise the banks, the government agency Fondo Bancario de Protección al Ahorro borrowed from the central bank and bought subordinated debt (convertible into common shares) from the banks.[24] This process is similar that of granting the ESM a banking licence so that it can use central bank financing to purchase euro-zone bank equity or government debt, instead of relying on issuing debt to investors. Resistance to this policy remains high.

A lesson from these emerging market stories is that economic and financial conditions improve rapidly once the authorities have dealt with their sovereign debt and bank problems. This means a quick break-up of the euro currency union would be beneficial because it would force a significant amount of the necessary sovereign debt and bank restructuring in the minimum amount of time. Currency parities would reflect national cost structures and so iron out differentials in competitiveness, thereby correcting chronic current-account imbalances.

Defaults could clear bank balance sheets of toxic assets, foreign-currency liabilities could be renegotiated, making liabilities denominated in the new devalued currencies affordable, and national central banks would be able to provide any liquidity support the domestic banking system may need. Governments would borrow from their central banks to recapitalise their commercial banks. The newly capitalised banks would be able to make the loans needed to fund recovery.

The decline and fall of banks

Throughout the crisis, policymakers have tried their utmost to prevent holders of government debt from taking losses, with the Greek restructuring the only major capitulation in this sense. Irish bank subordinated bondholders were forced to take substantial losses, but otherwise only equity holders and taxpayers have really had to pay so far. More recently, investors in the most troubled Spanish banks have been asked to bear losses as part of the first round of ESM-led recapitalisations. However, when the necessary write-downs are taken on European government and financial debts, some senior bank bondholders probably will take losses, the recent legislation protecting them to 1 January 2018 notwithstanding, as sufficient equity or government credit to absorb these losses is unlikely to be available. Some bondholders could receive equity in exchange for their bonds and the lucky ones will recoup their losses over time.

Banks, especially European banks, have relied far too much on liability management to fund their operations. The unending parade of bank crises throughout the history of fractional banking attests to the risk in plain vanilla banking. Investment banking multiplies that risk. In fact, investment banking is so risky that all investment banks were partnerships or very closely held private companies until the New York Stock exchange ended its prohibition of member firms incorporating in 1970. That was soon after the opening of the Eurodollar market, and Regulation Q capping the interest rates that banks were allowed to pay on deposits enabled large-scale liability management by commercial banks.

Limited liability for investment banks and liability management for commercial banks completely transformed modern banking. The traditional banker disdain for risk became avid risk seeking. The result of this change, a series of escalating bank crises, was perfectly predictable: the Latin American crises, the savings and loan crisis, the Asian crisis, the Long-Term Capital Management default, the Russian crisis, the subprime mortgage crisis and the coming European sovereign debt/banking crisis.

The only surprise is that the credit structure survived so many crises intact enough for most people to believe that nothing significant had changed since the AIG/Lehman default. A euro break-up would correct that misconception. Banks are often considered less creditworthy than non-financial companies: the highest S&P rating for any US bank is AA–. Falling ratings would raise their cost of capital and banks would find it much more expensive to secure funding in a post-euro future. Investors would demand greater compensation for risk when buying unsecured bank debt. The rising cost of funds would curtail liability management over time. As governments are also less creditworthy than some non-financial companies, government guarantees of the banking sector would be worth less, so would not lower the cost of non-deposit liabilities as much as they used to.

US banks have already sharply reduced their dependence on the credit markets for funding – credit-market instruments as a percentage of total liabilities reached over 8% in 2007, but have since fallen back to 3.4% as banks have turned increasingly to short-term deposits (helped by temporary unlimited Federal Deposit Insurance Corporation insurance on corporate deposits, which has now expired). Even so, cash-rich companies are funding the US banking system by parking their spare resources in low-interest-rate accounts, but that money has begun to trickle out. Small-time and savings deposits, which reached over 50% of banks' total liabilities in 2010, should take up some of the slack as interest rates rise, but US bank balance sheets may shrink.

Meanwhile, deposits were only 41% of euro-zone banks' liabilities in 2006 compared with 53% in 1995. Marketable credit instruments (loans and securities other than shares) represented 24%. Most of the balance was wholesale funding. More limited and expensive wholesale funding and higher capital ratios guarantee that European bank balance sheets will continue to shrink – hopefully enough to help defuse the too-big-to-fail problem and move banks back to their proper roles of distributing saving to those who can best use it. This is an inherently risky business because it involves mismatched terms. Banks take deposits (borrow short) and lend long. The risk in investment banking is underwriting the debt and equity issues that fund business activity. A fully functioning capitalist economy needs banks to perform these two functions. Adding to these two functions needlessly increases risk and should be prohibited in a risk-averse future.

The post-war Minsky cycle

The post-war period has traced the three stages of the Minsky cycle, from hedge to speculative to Ponzi finance (see Chapter 1). In the last stage, Ponzi, new debt must be taken out to pay the interest on existing debt, raising the ratio of debt to assets – the situation in which the troubled euro-zone economies find themselves. Taking on added debt to pay the interest on existing debt always results in default, so the coming euro crisis should force a major restructuring of many European companies and return the corporate sector to hedge financing. By contrast, most companies in the US and UK have strong enough balance sheets to weather the storm and invest profitably in the recovery, because the 2001–02 and 2007–09 recessions eliminated much of their Ponzi debt.

In the 1950s, US corporate financing was basically the hedge model, with companies able to pay down debts from cash flow via the then mandatory sinking funds (the annual repurchase of part of each bond issue). In years where cash flow more than covered capital expenditures and sinking funds, corporations paid down loans (1949, 1954, 1958). In the UK, BP was self-financing from 1929 until the mid-1950s. Aggressive investment plans led to the company's first post-war rights issue in 1966, followed by various bank loan agreements. Indeed, such was the reliance by large companies on internal finance, the treasury function only really developed in UK companies in the 1960s and 1970s.[25]

US companies made widespread use of equity financing between 1946 and 1970. From then on, debt financing took increasing precedence. Speculation began to creep into corporate funding in the early 1960s, when the commercial paper market began to take off as firms in the US and UK took the opportunity to raise cheap, short-term finance through the money markets. Although still a small proportion of overall liabilities, the stock of non-financial corporate commercial paper rose from $1 billion in 1960 to $7 billion in 1970. Five commercial paper defaults occurred in the US in the 1960s, totalling $35 million. In 1970, the Penn Central Transportation Company default on $83 million of commercial paper shocked the market. Fed support through the discount window and the raising of interest-rate ceilings on bank certificates of deposit allowed banks to provide liquidity support to companies having difficulty rolling over their commercial paper.[26] This was the first Minsky credit bubble collapse.

The end of the Bretton Woods system in 1971 and greater geographical diversification by large companies encouraged the development of the Eurodollar market and created a need for companies to hedge their foreign-currency exposure.[27] The early 1970s also saw the development of floating-rate loans when the First National City Bank of New York initiated a policy of resetting its prime rate every week based on a three-week moving average of money market rates. This reduction of interest-rate risk meant that banks had to hold less capital against floating-rate loans while corporations needed to manage these risks for the first time.[28]

The Chicago Mercantile Exchange and the Chicago Board of Trade launched currency futures in 1972 and interest-rate futures in 1975 to meet the demand for instruments to hedge the new currency and interest-rate risks while dependence on speculative forms of funding increased rollover risk. The failure of Herstatt bank in 1974 highlighted the increasing counterparty risk in the newly developed foreign-exchange markets and the new dangers of the evolving speculative financial system.

High bank lending rates and rising inflation in the 1970s pushed companies towards issuing corporate bonds and commercial paper. The availability of cheap corporate debt financing and the extremely favourable tax treatment of debt interest allowed leveraged buyouts (LBOs) to generate huge returns from purchasing companies with little equity investment, lumbering them with huge amounts of debt, thereby deliberately creating below-investment-grade bonds – appropriately labelled junk bonds. The conventional wisdom of the day was that junk bonds would pay their principal and interest as long there was no recession before they matured. Private equity and Ponzi finance had begun.

Figure 19   **US prime lending rate**
%

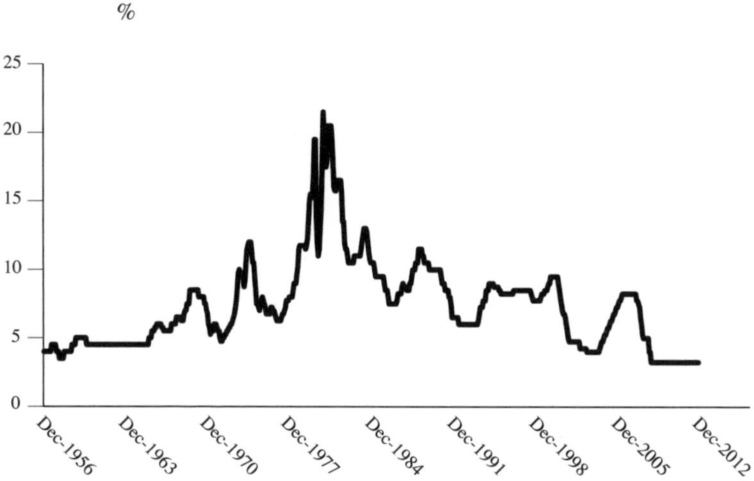

Source: Datastream

Surprisingly, investors' fear of credit risk disappeared, the market for junk bonds took off and the number of LBOs soared. LBOs greatly increased leverage and, worse, the threat of becoming an LBO target induced potential targets to leverage up themselves.

Commercial paper was usually guaranteed by bank lines of credit following the Penn Central Transportation Company bankruptcy. If the company could not roll over its commercial paper, it could draw on its line of credit to do so. However, after the credit downgrades of Integrated Resources and the Mortgage Realty Trust, banks withdrew their lines of credit from troubled corporations, which led to a series of commercial paper defaults in 1989–91. Chrysler Financial also found itself unable to access the commercial paper market in the 1990s.[29]

Furthermore, deregulation of the savings and loan industry had allowed non-bank financial institutions to compete for funding, raising its cost and encouraging these institutions to seek riskier lending opportunities, especially in real estate and junk bonds. Losses on these investments put about a quarter of US savings and loan institutions into bankruptcy in the late 1980s and early 1990s. The Financial Institutions Reform, Recovery and Enforcement Act of 1989 forced the savings and loan institutions to sell all their below-investment-grade bonds, shutting down the junk bond market, albeit temporarily. This was the second Minsky credit bubble collapse.

Exposing the Ponzi scheme

The collapse of speculative/Ponzi finance was many times worse than the collapse of hedge/speculative finance, but no lessons were learned, so the credit system progressed to pure Ponzi finance – the securitisation of real-estate loans. Excess lending to real estate and the development of interest-only and negative-amortising products were clear indicators that Ponzi finance was dominant. When a company borrows to invest in a productive asset, the cash flows generated by that asset can pay the interest and amortise the loan. When securing a loan against a property, the borrower has to pay the interest and amortise the loan from other sources of income. If other sources of income are inadequate, house prices must keep rising to prevent defaults.

Securitisation removed the credit risk of real-estate lending from the lenders' balance sheets while providing them with two sources of income: the profits on the sale of the mortgages and the steady income from servicing them. As a result, lenders stopped worrying about the borrowers' incomes and the values of their homes and concentrated on the volume of loans they could create for sale to off-balance-sheet entities that securitised and resold them. No longer did it matter whether borrowers could ultimately pay their debts or if the homes could be sold to recoup the defaulted debts. The securitising entities bridged the gap from their purchases of the mortgages and the sale of the securitised debt with short-term money market loans backed by the implicit guarantees of their parent banks.

Real-estate prices began to fall in 2006, dooming this Ponzi scheme. The subprime mortgage fiasco in 2007 led to the AIG/Lehman Brothers collapse. Banks and companies relied on money market funds, which were able to offer higher returns and guarantee no loss of capital, rolling over their commercial paper to keep the US financial system liquid. The Reserve Primary Funds' inability to redeem its shares at $1 escalated the Lehman Brothers bankruptcy to a major financial crisis, triggering a run on similar funds.[30] This was the US Minsky moment. Only an unprecedented two-and-a-half times expansion of the Fed's balance sheet plus Treasury deficits ranging up to an amazing $1.5 trillion prevented the real-estate collapse from plunging the US into deflation. Whether the debt these record-breaking initiatives created is viable will be known only after Europe goes through its Minsky moment: the break-up of the euro zone.

Corporate salvation

The US effort to prevent its Ponzi debt from collapsing into deflation and depression shifted debt from the private sector to the public sector. Taking the toxic structured debt onto public balance sheets has greatly reduced Ponzi finance in the US. By contrast, peripheral states in the euro zone are in a depression that is spreading and ECB liquidity has been unleashed to sustain the increasing government debt as governments must keep issuing new debt to pay not only the interest on their old debts but also part of their running costs – Ponzi debt writ large.

A euro-zone break-up is the one thing that could put its former member states into recovery. Sustainable, long-term recovery could occur within 24 months of the break-up if governments recapitalise their banks properly and restructure themselves to enable private-sector growth. Although some corporate sectors are in serious trouble (Portugal, Ireland, Spain and Italy), others appear reasonably healthy and have low leverage. They should be able to survive the welter of defaults and currency devaluations and revaluations and be in the vanguard of the European recovery.

Normally, the financial sector must be stabilised before recovery can begin, but that may not be necessary in the current cycle. The US, UK and Japanese non-financial corporate sectors are flush with cash, with savings exceeding investment by a substantial margin. Moreover, not only have emerging country companies been gaining market share, but they will also be less affected by the European sovereign debt/banking crisis than developed country companies. While governments and households have been busily borrowing from the future to fund spending today, companies in the US, UK, Japan and other countries have been doing the opposite – saving instead of spending. As a result, many of these companies should have strong enough balance sheets to fund the investment needed for future growth without recourse to

Figure 20   **US and EU-17 non-financial corporations: loans/total liabilities**
%

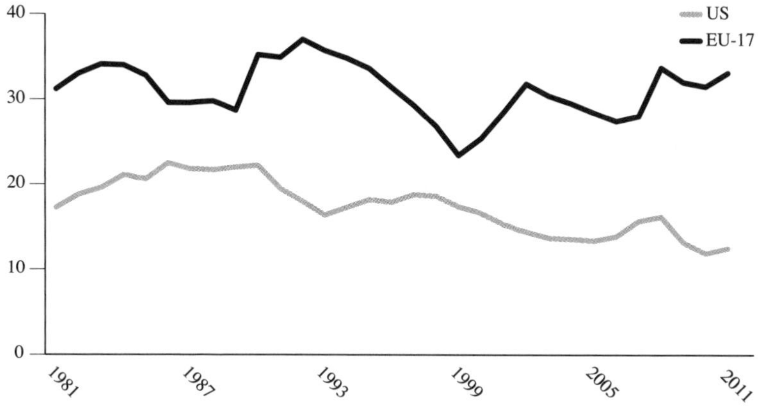

Sources: US Federal Reserve; Eurostat

bank loans. Figure 20 shows that US dependence on bank funding has dropped sharply and is likely to continue to do so.

By contrast, European non-financial companies depend much more on bank funding than their US counterparts. However, bank lending to the private sector is already contracting, even before the debt crisis has fully run its course, forcing European companies to rely more heavily on the capital markets to fund their activities. Greater equity issuance and more corporate bonds will lead to better yields for investors. Once the necessary debt write-offs have taken place, foreign companies are likely to take advantage of the cheap European investment opportunities on offer.

Bank lending will have to await recapitalisation, but healthy companies need not depend on banks as they will be able to fund themselves cheaply in capital markets. Standard & Poor's still rates Johnson & Johnson and ExxonMobil AAA, higher than the US Treasury, and premiums on corporate credit default swaps often drop below those for the US sovereign, especially in defensive equity sectors such as consumer staples and healthcare. Meanwhile, yields on corporate debt are still much higher than sovereign yields, offering substantial risk-adjusted returns to investors. In addition, the commercial paper market often offers cheaper funding than taking out short-term loans from banks.[31]

US non-financial corporations have been net buyers of equity for the past 18 years. Since 2009, US companies have been able to fund almost their entire investment needs with internal funds, as the $1.1 trillion of net corporate debt issuance in the 2009–11 period has almost been matched by $800 billion of net equity retirement. Paying executives with equity options has made US corporations adopt large-scale share buy-back schemes since the early 1990s. Established companies have generally been investing less than their cash flow in recent years, so winding down share buy-backs will end unnecessary use of leverage by non-financial corporations and the transition to the safety of hedge financing will be complete.

A euro-zone break-up would reduce world trade and the cash flows of companies. US company earnings from Europe would take a hit, putting pressure on retained profits, but even a $200 billion aggregate loss (one-sixth of total internal funds) would leave current capital expenditures fully covered by internal resources. An end to large-scale share buy-backs would free up further resources. Even so, the 24-month global recession after the euro-zone break-up would probably squeeze cash flow enough to reverse the three decades of US corporations persistently buying back shares. And the unwinding of the Eurasian savings glut would raise real interest rates.

Excess corporate cash flow would fall too, partly through lower earnings in the euro-zone break-up recession, partly through higher capital costs and partly through higher investment. Developed countries' economies and financial patterns in the post-break-up recession recovery would resemble the North American ones in the 1950s and 1960s, with investment leading the way up. The next chapter will show how emerging countries should lead the recovery. Growth in their domestic demand would boost exports from developed countries, spurring investment (especially in cutting-edge technology) and satisfying two of the requirements for recovery, which will help developed countries recover from their somewhat deeper and longer recessions.

Exports growing faster than imports and rising investment are two signs of permanent recovery from banking crises. Preceding chapters have discussed the need for restructuring the financial system and government. This chapter has shown that a euro-zone break-up would rid the world of a substantial amount of its toxic debt, and that changes in non-financial corporation funding have made banks virtually redundant in their main function, which is transferring saving from savers to those who can make the best use of saving. Thus events are forcing much of the needed financial restructuring. Chapter 10 will pursue this theme and discuss the restructuring of government and the monetary system.

10

The required restructuring

The global economy and financial markets have entered a critical state; in physics, this is the state of a substance in which the gaseous and liquid phases have the same temperature, pressure and volume. Upon approaching the critical state, the physical properties of substances undergo sharp changes because regions of instability proliferate. Reactions to external forces become unpredictable as substances near the critical state, then stabilise again as the new form gains dominance and reduces regions of instability. Economies and financial markets behave in a similar way.

In credit bubbles, rising leverage increases the probability of bankruptcy, making the economy and financial markets markedly more unstable. As is true of all critical states, this instability can result in one of two outcomes. Printing enough money to keep the economy liquid, albeit ever more insolvent, may cause hyperinflation; or the rising insolvency may burst the credit bubble, causing deflation. The only outcome that cannot possibly occur is the one that politicians, bureaucrats and financial markets desperately want – printing enough money to borrow our way out of insolvency.

Hyperinflation usually occurs in a country because the only

way to keep borrowing rising enough to maintain the upward spiral in credit in the face of soaring interest rates and a collapsing economy is to keep borrowing ever more money to export out of the country. Ergo, hyperinflation requires a plummeting exchange rate, which, in turn, needs a stock of foreign assets, usually mostly currency, large and liquid enough to easily accommodate all the money fleeing the collapsing economy. This makes a global hyperinflation a contradiction in terms. A US dollar hyperinflation is equally impossible because there is no set of assets big enough to absorb a global flight of US dollars. Government borrowing has nullified the private sector's attempts to delever in all but the US and Japan, although Italy has delevered slightly. Developed countries must delever more and deleverage causes deflation, regardless of how aggressively central banks expand their balance sheets.

This book has shown that a widespread deflation is virtually guaranteed. Global financial systems are riddled with bad debt. Fiscal deficits and printing money are increasing the amount of bad debt every day. Moving bad private debt onto public balance sheets merely trashes the public balance sheets. Restructuring bad debt is no solution either; most of it defaults again within a year. These 'fixes' have prevented the subprime crisis, which, in any past period, would have begun the necessary deleveraging process, from accomplishing anything.

Total global leverage is greater today than it was in 2007 when the subprime crisis hit. The too-big-to-fail banks (TBTF) are bigger than ever and many are now literally too big to bail out. They will take their sovereigns down with them. European banks are both more highly levered and more stuffed with bad loans than in 2007. The proportion of ratings with negative outlooks doubled in the first half of 2012 in several categories, mainly due to shocks from the euro zone.

Monetary stimulation has boosted asset markets but has been ineffective in its primary task of increasing growth. Interest rates at the zero bound have eased the cost of servicing debts, but cannot reduce debt as a proportion of assets without output growing faster than the rate of interest. That could occur if investment and/or consumption rose fast enough, but this is not happening because the mechanism that converts bank reserves into money is broken for reasons explained in detail in Chapter 4.

Furthermore, bank equity is inadequate and credit worries are reducing wholesale funding. JPMorgan, Goldman Sachs and Black Rock have closed their European money market funds to new investors as the low rates jeopardise returns to existing investors. Lack of equity is shrinking loans in European banks, reducing growth in the money supply, and the Eurasian savings glut is reversing. Lower interest rates can delay default, but cannot produce credit growth in a period of falling incomes and deleverage. Expanding central bank balance sheets prevent liquidity-driven banking collapse, but cannot generate GDP growth.

Real interest rates are rising as inflation falls and European bank problems are sending companies into the bond market. The only positive in the savings, investment and interest-rate picture is that non-financial companies' overinvestment in the past is piling up cash on their balance sheets. The outlook for fiscal stimulation is no better. Economists have lowered their global growth forecasts significantly and 2013 should still disappoint. As a result, automatic stabilisers threaten to raise the already egregious fiscal deficits and sovereign debts alarmingly. Growth high enough to escape debt traps is virtually impossible. Worse, the European sovereign debt/banking crisis puts all the errors on the downside.

The European slowdown spread to China, which had a deflationary hard landing that reduced growth in the rest of Asia. Suddenly, the US has become the hope for the future, but is that hope realistic? None of the National Bureau of Economic Research (NBER) indicators (payroll employment, real personal income less transfers, real manufacturing and wholesale sales, industrial production) has crested the 2007 high. This means that the heart of the US economy is still mired in the last recession, even though the GDP figures indicate recovery.

Investors.com reported that enrolments in the Social Security Insurance Disability programme since the low in June 2009 grew by 4.7 million – compared with growth of 2.3 million in non-farm payroll employment.[32] This subsidy to consumers also subsidises imports, and the trade deficit increased sharply in late 2012. This suggests that the NBER indicators are telling the true story, and that the residue of the fiscal cliff left after the panic negotiations at the end of 2012 will probably push the US into recession in 2013.

As a result, financial markets now depend on the continuous monetary expansion that people believe will enable muddling through to a time when some unspecified change will enable adequate growth and/or inflation. That belief would be justified if the problem was liquidity, but the world is floating on a sea of liquidity. The problem is a lack of capital, which prevents excess liquidity from supporting new lending. The zero risk weighting on government debt means that excess liquidity finds its way into sovereign debt, reinforcing the link between banks and governments.

This cannot produce growth, but it does keep raising leverage and boosting asset prices, which are greatly hindering developed country recoveries from the Great Recession. Commodities and energy are now assets and printing money has raised their prices faster than incomes, so real incomes are falling. A record 46.5 million Americans are on the food stamp programme and austerity and money printing have pushed incomes so low in peripheral Europe that Unilever is changing its market strategies to cater for the increasing poverty.[33]

Populations are ageing, risk aversion is rising and ever more highly indebted entities are becoming insolvent. The problem is too much debt and too little equity. Printing money does nothing to solve that problem because it creates additional debt equal to the amount of money printed. With many borrowers insolvent, printing money is merely adding to the bad debt that must ultimately be written off, as has already happened with Greek debt. Meanwhile, monetary conditions remain extremely tight because private-sector credit is not growing fast enough, if at all.

Financial markets are starting to recognise the limits of money printing, so co-ordinated credit easing has moved them little. With interest rates at historic lows, the only way that printed money could even postpone the inevitable deflation in developed countries is for central banks to buy toxic assets from banks at book cost. This would temporarily ease the severe capital squeeze that is forcing most European banks to shrink their private-sector loans and taxpayers would not have to pay the resulting losses until the crisis hits. Fortunately, this futile effort at postponing the inevitable is not on anyone's agenda – yet.

Chapter 4 explained why the only way to make European banks viable again is to recapitalise them. Lack of wholesale funding in the absence of ECB intervention means the wide gap between their loans and their deposits would ultimately force banks to shrink their balance sheets. Even so, writing off the hidden losses on their balance sheets would make the required amounts of new capital enormous. Core states can borrow enough to recapitalise their banks properly, but the only ways to recapitalise peripheral state banks are by borrowing trillions of euros through the ESM or by exiting the euro and recapitalising banks in the devalued local currency.

As a result, the only solutions to the European sovereign debt/ banking crisis are either rapid progress in creating a credible path to fiscal and political union or a euro break-up. The politicians' and pundits' calls for more union are occurring as member states are drifting apart. Printing money is effectively widening the gap, so break-up is by far the most likely outcome – and the most positive outcome. It would instantly correct the economic problems and the current-account imbalances, and it would force reluctant governments to write off the bad debts and recapitalise the financial system. Correcting these two problems would set the stage for sustainable recovery.

Credit expansion borrowed output and income from the future for about four decades. That future has now arrived and rendered the printing presses useless. We can neither go back and undo the mistakes of the past nor evade paying the price for them. Unfortunately, human beings are hard-wired to put off pain – even when they know putting it off will make it far worse. Our ever more elaborate efforts to postpone pain are formidable, but the four-decade-and-counting accumulation of pain is growing even more formidable and pushing the euro zone into consolidation or break-up. Both would force a restructuring of banks.

Restructuring banks

This book has dwelt on bank problems, the power of the bank lobby to stall, prevent or emasculate reform and what governments are (not) doing to circumvent the banking lobby. The problems with banks are many and complex. They are inhibiting growth and costing taxpayers billions while bankers earn grotesquely huge incomes and governments wring their hands, weep crocodile tears and remain staunchly on the sidelines. Most people consider Europe to be the biggest threat to banks, but derivatives are an even bigger threat. The Bank of International Settlements' calculation of the notional amount of derivatives outstanding was just over $700 trillion, about ten times global GDP, at the end of 2011. Most people content themselves with the thought that netting reduces that figure by about 90% to one times global GDP, with about 70% being plain vanilla interest-rate contracts that embody little capital risk.

The bad news is that netting ignores counterparty risk: the risk that one of the parties to a contract will not fulfil its obligations. Counterparty risk bankrupted Bear Stearns and Lehman Brothers in 2008, and the concurrent failure of AIG to fulfil its commitments would have caused a tsunami of failures and deflation – had the US Treasury not underwritten its liabilities. Global bank assets may exceed GDP by about 50% and the notional value of derivatives on TBTF banks dwarf their monetary assets, maybe by seven times.

Unfortunately, the losses on virtual assets cost real money. The last banking crisis has trashed sovereign balance sheets, so trouble in virtual banking would bankrupt most developed country banks. Worse, banks have abused the implicit government subsidy to grow their derivatives businesses – 99% of JPMorgan's $79 trillion derivatives book is housed within its deposit-taking subsidiary.[34] The good news is the European sovereign debt/banking crisis should automatically reform and recapitalise banks by turning too-big-to-fail into too-big-to-bail-out.

Most governments and central banks entered the last banking crisis with strong balance sheets and considerable latitude for stimulation. By contrast, monetary stimulation is now non-productive and fiscal stimulation impossible due to massive fiscal deficits and soaring debt-to-GDP ratios. Interest rates are already close to or at the zero bound, real interest rates should rise as inflation falls, the mechanism that converts bank reserves into money is broken, private-sector credit is shrinking in many countries, growth in global money supplies has slowed and the Eurasian savings glut is reversing. European bank problems are sending companies into the bond market.

Some countries are in a far worse condition than others, but all have suffered a massive decline in their scope to stimulate when the crisis hits. A collapse of the euro should force a comprehensive restructuring of European banking systems. The failure of one or more TBTF banks bankrupting a government or two would certainly crush the power of the bank lobby and so hasten the implementation of badly needed structural bank reform. The US, unlike many European countries, can still restructure and recapitalise its banking system without nationalising it.

One of those reforms should be banning cash settlement of derivatives. Ending the requirement to deliver the underlying asset enabled the explosion of derivatives contracts that allowed the derivatives tail to wag the cash market dog. Derivatives have also created yet more unnecessary risk for unsophisticated companies and public bodies, just as the development of floating-rate loans in the 1970s exposed them to new interest-rate risks. Inappropriate sales of derivates to small and medium-sized companies have created a scandal in the UK, and public bodies in the US are suing investment banks over the same issue.

Reimposing the ban would end the ridiculously costly situation of derivatives determining cash prices and return derivatives to their economic function of hedging risk. Even if the authorities act slowly, the decimation of bank balance sheets and the rediscovered risk that failure will unseat the management of any bank should return banks to the high degree of risk avoidance that characterised the early post-war banks. Few insolvent banks can survive, so the fear of bankruptcy can discipline banks. Unfortunately, the same is not true of governments.

Governments and central banks

Chapter 6 provided a brief outline of the role of government, and when and where it should intervene in society. It is impossible to give a full assessment of how to reform all areas of government activity in this book, but what we can do is offer practical suggestions for government to live within its means. A sensible approach would be to define the types of activities government should undertake in conjunction with a broad restriction on the size of government relative to the economy. At what point does increased government activity stop facilitating better growth and private-sector gains, and start to become a drag on growth, welfare and the private sector?

Once society has prioritised which types of activities it would

like government to perform and how, defining a maximum size
of government as a proportion of GDP is one means of keeping
excessive or wasteful spending in check. A basic message of
Daron Acemoglu and James A. Robinson's book *Why Nations
Fail: The Origins of Power, Prosperity and Poverty*[35] is that
civilisations collapse after their governments become too big
and powerful. How big is too big? Before the First World War,
most governments spent 10% of GDP or less in peacetime. A
variety of studies have shown that the optimal size of governments is about 20% of GDP or less. Government spending in
most developed countries now ranges from 36% to 55% of GDP.
On this basis, they are all too big. To a certain extent, however,
the size of government itself is not important; whether government is undertaking productive, welfare-enhancing activities is
the more important issue, but also much more difficult to define.
A simple debt-ceiling-type arrangement at least provides protection to voters from government largesse.

Government spending was 10% of GDP or less when the discipline of the gold standard limited global credit to global saving.
That percentage began to grow as soon as the monetary system
permitted credit to rise faster than saving, and government now
carries out far more activities than it did a century ago. Most
of these, such as the National Health Service in the UK, voters
would like to hold onto. The aim is not to revert to government at
10% of GDP, but to ask how government can carry out the kinds
of activities we want and need it to without the support of ever-
expanding central bank balance sheets, and without placing an
intolerable burden on ordinary taxpayers.

Most people think government must live within its means, just
like they and their businesses, and even banks, must ultimately

do. Not so. Most governments have central banks that can and do buy their bonds, so insolvency is no impediment to their continuing to live far beyond their means until hyperinflation or a credit collapse ends the party. Even then, the restructuring of government required to avoid a repetition of the calamity is far from certain.

An increase in the government deficit must be matched by an increase in savings in the other sectors (household, corporate or foreign), as the balance of savings and investment in all four sectors must sum to zero (see Chapter 3). Increased government spending therefore reduces spending in the other sectors by reducing incomes through taxes or by private-sector funding of deficits. Governments need credit in excess of saving to increase their share of GDP. Degrading their currencies was essential to their ability to quadruple or quintuple their share of GDP in the last century. As a result, the purchasing power of the dollar and sterling have fallen by 95% since 1912 – the most comprehensive degradation of reserve and former reserve currencies in history – even though the period encompassed the worst deflation/depression since the Industrial Revolution began. Restoring sound money is an essential part of restructuring government.

It has been too easy for governments to expand their activities beyond what is useful and welfare-enhancing, facilitated by the rapid growth of central bank balance sheets and easy credit. A possible solution to this problem would be to isolate central banks from governments. The supposed independence of central banks has been revealed as a fallacy to the public by increased central bank purchases of government bonds as part of crisis-fighting measures, although central banks keeping interest rates far too low long before the financial crisis should have been a clue. Co-operation between the new central banks and governments of countries leaving the euro would be essential to recapitalise banks after exit, but a better system is needed to prevent governments and central banks from going back to their old ways of inflating and devaluing.

Separating central banks and governments is almost impossible under current conditions. Typically, central banks, such as the Fed, have hedged balance sheets. Prime-quality short-term interest-bearing paper hedges their monetary liabilities and they have the further backstop of a call on the national treasury in the event of negative net worth. This guarantees the instant conversion of maturing sovereign bonds into cash. Moreover, the sovereign can always borrow from the central bank, so it is always liquid regardless of its solvency.

The ECB could provide a template for better central banks in the future. Like the Bank of England for most of its history, the ECB operates more like a commercial bank. It does not have a hedged balance sheet, the backstop of a national treasury or the authority to buy bonds directly from governments. It cannot be turned into a Fed-type central bank until it has all three. Thus it cannot guarantee the immediate conversion of maturing sovereign bonds into cash, so no incestuous relationship exists between it and the national governments, which should limit the growth of governments. The downside of this arrangement is that the ECB cannot be the lender of last resort to European sovereign borrowers until both fiscal union occurs and the EU amends its charter to turn it into a Fed-type central bank. Inability to buy bonds directly from a government means it could not have prevented the Greek default and will not be able to prevent any future sovereign default.

As discussed in Chapter 6, interest rates are better used as a barometer of economic conditions than as a policy tool. Using interest rates as a signal, the central bank balance sheet could expand and contract through the economic cycle – monetary, rather than fiscal, automatic stabilisers. In periods of acute recession and financial crisis, aggressive central bank balance sheet expansion would be justified to keep money supply growing and ease pressures on nominal GDP. This differs greatly from the excessively cosy relationship that underpinned the growth of government and the 95% or more depreciation of currencies in the last century. The leap from central bank balance sheets expanding and contracting in response to freely floating interest rates to the old automatic stabilisers of the gold standard is not a great one (more on this later).

The multitudinous discussions on reforming government going on in Europe and North America do not include the optimal size of government, or how to prioritise spending, or the efficiency of various forms of taxation. The discussions also ignore the many idiocies embedded in tax laws. A flagrant idiocy in the tax laws of many developed countries allows companies to deduct interest payments from taxable income, but not dividends. Action to change this finally emerged in the French budget in September 2012, which cut the tax relief on corporate interest payments.

Debt provides lower-cost funding and has bankrupted a vast number of companies throughout history; equity funding costs more and has never bankrupted a company. The lower-cost dangerous funding is not taxed and the higher-cost completely safe funding is double taxed. Disallowing the deduction of interest paid in excess of interest received and permitting companies to deduct dividends paid out of income earned in the current tax year would promote much stronger corporate balance sheets and end the unfairness of double-taxing the safest form of corporate funding.

Furthermore, the discussions fail to talk about ways to improve fiscal policy, such as cyclical budgeting, which would:

- raise government accounting to the sophisticated level required of private companies;
- set an inviolate proportion of GDP for average government spending including capital investment;
- administer the capital budget counter-cyclically.

Cyclical budgeting would help governments live within their means. Governments should prioritise spending so that the total share of GDP remains constant. Prioritising spending would force every department to defend every expenditure item every year, rewarding the leaders of programmes that underspend and punishing the leaders of those that overspend. Departments would have to defend each current expenditure item annually, but the budget process should cover a complete cycle, allocating capital spending in such a way that the surpluses and deficits over a complete business cycle total zero. The next step is to create a tax regime with the least adverse economic impact.

Investment, not consumption, drives capitalist economies, making infrastructure spending governments' most powerful weapon to stimulate their economies. However, the accounting systems that most governments use are not sophisticated enough to calculate the return on money spent. Best-practice accounting would show the return on most government programmes is negative, which is why fiscal stimulation yields such poor returns.

Public capital spending on projects with positive returns admin-
istered to rise as private capital spending falls and fall as private
capital spending rises would vastly outperform the present arcane
welter of automatic stabilisers and policy on the hoof. With interest rates so low, there would be plenty of available projects. Of
course, if steps one and two had been taken a few decades ago, a
lot of governments would have avoided the trouble they are now
in without ever needing step three.

Instead, the discussions centre on secondary questions, such
as whether the rich are paying their fair share, without a single
criterion to guide the discussion. In the US, where this discussion
is probably most heated, the top 1% (1.4 million taxpayers) earns
20% of the income and pays 38% of income taxes. The bottom
half (70 million taxpayers) earns 12½% of income and pays 2½%
of income taxes. Do these figures favour the 70 million over the
1.4 million, or vice versa? We have no idea, but comparisons
with other countries indicate that US income differentials are relatively wide, so the rise in taxes as a percentage of income should
be correspondingly steep.

The tax regime should be reformed to have the least adverse
economic impact. Income taxes are a highly inefficient way to
raise revenues, but the overall system of benefits and income taxes
makes a poor solution even worse. For individuals just on the cusp
of where benefits end and taxes start, the lack of a uniform system
can create high marginal tax rates as tax credits are withdrawn
and discourage re-entry into the labour force. Milton Friedman,
in his book *Capitalism and Freedom* (1962), proposed a 'negative income tax' – a flat rate of tax combined with tax allowances
where families above a certain threshold pay a constant propor-
tional rate of tax and families below a certain threshold receive a

rebate. For example, if the allowance was $20,000 and the linear rate of tax was 50%, a family earning $40,000 would pay $10,000 tax and a family earning $15,000 would receive a $2,500 rebate. Trials of such a system in New Jersey were ultimately unsuccessful, partly because the median income was too close to the poverty line, making the scheme too expensive.[36]

Income taxes reduce the incomes of workers and suppliers of goods and increase the costs of the goods and services they produce, lowering both the incentive to work and competitiveness. Consumption taxes, such as sales taxes, luxury taxes, import duties and value-added taxes are more efficient as they hit only once rather than twice. Land is the only non-moveable asset, and land-value taxes are both the most overlooked source of revenue and the only taxes that do not distort economic decisions.

Taxing labour, buildings, machinery and plant reduces beneficial activities, but land-value taxes do not because the tax is the same regardless of how the land is used. Land rents depend on what tenants will pay, not on the expenses of landlords, so land-value taxes cannot be directly passed on to tenants. Imposing a land-value tax deters speculative land holding, and so promotes the redevelopment of rundown inner-city areas. Unfortunately, landowners with significant political influence have consistently prevented the adoption of land-value taxes.

Politicians have always preferred raising taxes to cutting spending. James Tobin proposed a currency transaction tax be levied on all foreign-exchange transactions in 1971 as a way of limiting currency volatility. It proved unworkable and was dropped. Public anger against the so-called 'banksters' and 'black hole' fiscal deficits has revived interest in taxing financial institutions. As a result, European politicians have revived Tobin's tax in the form of a financial transactions tax of 0.1% on all stock, bond and derivative trades to:

- make banks repay a bit of what they have taken from the public;
- reduce speculation and financial engineering;
- create a fund to bail out banks that get into trouble in the future.

This sounds like a panacea for all financial problems. However, a tax of that magnitude on foreign-exchange futures would create a field day for the law of unintended consequences by raising the cost of commercial foreign-exchange transactions by between 1,000 and 10,000 times. A tax in Sweden of only 0.003% on transactions of bonds maturing in more than five years reduced the trading volume by 85%. Less trading increases market volatility (thereby decreasing confidence in markets) and lowers tax receipts far below estimates.

Even so, a financial transactions tax may be worthwhile. It would probably end an increasing scourge in modern financial markets, high-frequency trading, which not only is rapidly increasing needless volatility but also may be illegal because it more often than not front-runs client accounts. Unfortunately, bankers, especially investment bankers, worry little about the legality of their actions. Prosecutions are rare and have affected only minnows so far. A financial transactions tax would probably end high-frequency trading and rein in investment banks. Hobbling the two most destructive elements in financial markets may be worth all the problems and aggravation of designing and implementing a financial transactions tax.

Changing the way central banks operate by moving away from ad hoc policy decisions and towards a balance sheet which expands and contracts according to economic conditions (using free-moving interest rates as the barometer) would result in a system akin to the original gold standard, with its inherent automatic stabilisers. Returning to the gold standard would be a far more effective solution to this problem – and would also automatically prevent governments from growing too big.

The gold standard

The UK established a de facto gold standard in 1720 when the Bank of England began accumulating gold in the financial chaos generated by the collapses of the South Sea Bubble and the Mississippi Company. This was the first instance of a bank accumulating gold reserves against the notes (paper money) it issued and redeeming those notes for gold on demand. It created the most stable currency in the world, a significant factor in the Industrial Revolution starting in the UK.

The Bank of England suspended redemption during the Napoleonic Wars and printed too many notes. A *de jure* gold standard was instituted in 1816 with a higher price of gold (devalued paper money) to alleviate the post-war depression. The British system became international and evolved into the classic gold standard, which mandated:

- completely open capital accounts;
- settlement of international balances in gold;
- fixed bank reserve ratios;
- bank reserves be 100% gold;
- free convertibility between currency and gold at fixed rates.

Settling international balances in gold together with currency convertibility meant that countries with current-account deficits in excess of capital inflows automatically experienced deflationary gold outflows. The loss of gold triggered a rise in short-term rates and a fall in prices until the outflow stopped. Gold yields nothing, so rising short-term rates raised the opportunity cost of holding gold and public desire to hold it fell. Convertibility ensured the unwanted gold went into bank reserves, so they rose as investors converted gold into interest-bearing paper. Fixed bank reserve ratios meant a given flow of gold into banks would quickly increase the money supply, so the deflationary pressures soon ended.

Similarly, gold inflows increased bank reserves, triggering a drop in interest rates and a rise in prices. Falling short-term rates reduced the opportunity cost of holding gold, so rising public desire to hold gold quickly reduced bank reserves and the money supply, so the inflationary pressures soon ended. Also, a capital inflow greater than the current-account deficit had the same effect as a current-account surplus, and a capital outflow greater than the current-account surplus had the same effect as a current-account deficit. Gold flows forced frequent changes in short-term interest rates. For example, the Bank of England had to change the bank rate as many as 24 times in a year to keep the ratio of its gold reserves to its outstanding notes in a range consistent with maintaining free convertibility, although the odd year saw no change. Small interest-rate changes usually neutralised gold flows, thereby matching available capital with global investment needs.

Global trade under the classic gold standard was comparable to today, but purchasing power parities and real interest rates were more equal across the world than before or since. However, reserves were small, so flows had to be stopped quickly and big changes were sometimes needed. Crises did occur, but short-term interest rates quickly responded to conditions, correcting imbalances of saving and investment much faster than central banks can – and without political influence. As a result, under the gold standard recoveries occurred quickly, living standards rose faster and money performed its store of value function (unlike today).

Maintaining free convertibility and settling international balances in gold limited credit creation, preventing governments from pursuing inflationary policies. Zero long-term inflation kept long-term interest rates low and stable. From 1843 to 1914, British long bond yields ranged from a peak of 3.6% (in 1848) to a low of 2.4% (in 1895), making long-term planning easier. Countries (apart from the US) aborted the classic gold standard at the outbreak of the First World War, causing monetary chaos with a hodgepodge of open, partially open and closed capital accounts and fixed, floating and managed foreign-exchange rates. Worse, national monetary policies created inflation rates ranging from excessive to hyper.

In a misguided effort to sort the mess, the Genoa Conference in 1922 instituted the gold exchange standard, which tried to bring order to the monetary chaos, validate past inflation and enable future inflation. The dollar remained the only truly convertible currency. Others were not convertible into gold coins, only into large bars reserved for international transactions. Citizens could not exchange notes and securities for gold. The UK could hold foreign exchange and bank reserves in dollars and gold. Other countries could hold their reserves in dollars, sterling and gold.

The gold exchange standard did not restrict British balance-of-payments deficits and inflation because most other countries did not redeem their pounds for dollars or gold. Instead, they held the sterling as bank reserves and inflated their domestic money supplies accordingly, unleashing an inflationary boom in both the UK and Europe. Foreign exchange, most of it sterling, constituted 35% of European central bank reserves in 1930. In 1931, France tried to convert its sterling reserves into gold, but the UK did not have enough gold to comply and was forced off the gold exchange standard, collapsing this monetary system in less than a decade.

Irving Fisher and Hyman Minsky have explained that the only way to prevent credit bubbles from collapsing into deflation is to prevent the bubbles from forming. The secret of metal-based currencies is that unrestricted public convertibility in both directions embeds automatic stabilisers into the monetary system that prevent excessive credit creation. Monetary stability was a major factor in the UK's rise to world dominance in the 18th and 19th centuries and abandoning it contributed greatly to its fall in the 20th.

Convertible metal-based money creates the confidence needed to prosper in deflations. It helped drag the UK out of the post-Napoleonic Wars depression and the US out of the 1837 and 1873 depressions. By contrast, the post-First World War experience shows that fiddling with convertibility neuters the automatic stabilisers and the system collapses. No human-based system has ever approached the efficiency of the automatic stabilisers embedded into convertibility and the odds against one ever doing so are extremely long. The basic problem with the classic gold standard is that politicians often used the expense of war as an excuse to go off it.

Governments and banks thrive on inflation, and thus hate the gold standard. Even so, President Reagan appointed a Gold Commission to consider the feasibility of a metallic basis for the US currency in 1981. Donald Regan, Treasury secretary and a former CEO of Merrill Lynch, appointed the members, so favouring the continuation of fiat money was inevitable. However, the commission did recommend that another one be appointed in five years to re-examine the need to stabilise the value of the dollar. The Republicans revived the idea of a Gold Commission three decades and a 57% devaluation of the dollar later – to no avail.

Near-universal delusions about the omnipotent powers of credit, government and central banks would have kept the probability of a positive recommendation close to zero and, even if positive, the odds of politicians and political appointees constructing a successful metallic standard would have been equally small. A currency freely convertible into gold and/or silver could occur only after all else has failed to end the deflation/depression now spreading through Europe. Even so, tiny incremental steps towards that end can occur, such as the increasing use of gold as collateral and the Basel Committee considering whether to make gold a Tier 1 (zero risk-weighted) asset.

There is also talk of peripheral European countries backing their bonds with gold to lower interest rates in the same way that zero-coupon Treasuries backed defaulted Latin American bonds in the 1980s. This could be a first step towards gold-backed currencies. However, a new gold standard would probably originate in emerging countries. Turkey has effectively monetised gold domestically and its central bank is changing required gold reserves as a monetary policy tool. China is the global leader in gold production and is the second-largest gold importer, so it could easily mimic Turkey in monetising gold and continue towards a true gold standard. The huge public gold holdings in India make monetising attractive there too, but progress has been slow so far.

Gold-backed currencies in countries with adequate reserves and current accounts near balance, or receiving enough foreign direct investment to offset their current-account deficits, should be preferable to the dollar. This would give such countries the competitive advantage of relatively low interest rates. However, gold backing alone would not limit the government as it could keep reducing the gold backing – as the US did from the 40% mandated by the Bretton Woods Agreement until Nixon finally closed the gold window in 1971.

The difference between gold-backed currencies and the classic gold standard is unlimited convertibility, which is feasible only after bad debt has been purged from the financial system. As a result, the enormous and rising amounts of bad debt outstanding will probably prevent meaningful progress toward convertibility in developed countries until the European sovereign debt/banking crisis and its aftermath purges bad debt from the financial system. Purging the bad debt and downsizing governments should release the shackles on private-sector growth.

Downsizing governments

Chapter 3 introduced the idea that a lot of government spending can be counterproductive. One of the worst examples is business subsidies. Even though cutting corporate subsidies was a significant part of Canada's fiscal restructuring in the 1990s, a study by the Fraser Institute, *Corporate Welfare: Now a $182 Billion*

Addiction, found that government subsidies to failing businesses totalled about C$13,639 per taxpayer from 1995 to 2005. The institute argued that the bailouts only delayed the inevitable, hurting healthy companies because they merely created zombie companies that took business away from productive companies in the same industry. Governments can downsize, greatly reduce their deficits and enhance productivity and living standards simultaneously by eliminating business subsidies.

Subsidising business, especially manufacturing, is ridiculous as it is a major source of rising productivity. Business should be subsidising others, but the current keep-interest-rates-below-natural-rates policy (financial repression) has skewed the distribution of the benefits of rising productivity. It favours those closest to the money creation process, so governments, bankers and speculators profit at the expense of producers and most private-sector employees. Zombie companies are one result of this misallocation; excessive government pay is another.

US municipal employees receive 43% more in pay and benefits than private-sector workers doing essentially the same jobs[37] – and they have greater job security, an added non-monetary benefit that should hold public-sector monetary benefits below those of the private sector. Overpaid government employees and a history of less productivity indicate that the private sector could perform a number of the activities that governments have assumed over the past century better.

Private companies have four other advantages over public agencies. First, they can motivate employees better. Positive motivation includes the potentiality of wage increases not subject to bureaucratic restrictions and participation in profits. Negative motivation includes fear of dismissal for inefficiency and bankruptcy of the company. In the private sector incentives and sanctions are guaranteed, while the public sector is notorious for its propensity to duck, bob and weave. Second, the private sector has much greater flexibility in adjusting its resources (personnel, equipment and materials) to constantly changing situations. Third, private companies' long-term contracts can make effective trade-offs between investment, maintenance and operation costs as environmental, social and economic requirements change. Fourth, private companies keep investing in research and development to constantly improve the quality and efficiency of their techniques, processes and equipment.

Chapter 6 outlined some of the considerations, both ethical and economic, which come to bear on what governments should do, and how. The difficult economic backdrop and excess government debt provide an opportunity to reassess which activities take place in the public sector and which take place in the private sector. Some activities will take place more efficiently in the public sector, including the provision of public goods, but others the private sector can carry out more productively. The transition to the private sector has already begun, as it has been playing an increasing role in infrastructure and other government programmes through public/private initiatives. Typically, private firms are building public facilities, such as hospitals, prisons and roads, and either leasing them to or running them on behalf of public authorities for the duration of the contract. Ownership of the facilities passes to the public at the end of the contract.

Under the UK's private finance initiative (PFI), the government can commission a capital project from the private sector and then contract services from the asset for a certain number of years. This limits upfront capital expenditure and, happily for politicians, leaves the capital expenditure off balance sheet. But even these projects can fall foul of public-sector flaws. The National Audit Office reported that the data had not been collected in order to see whether PFI had led to better outcomes than other forms of procurement. A lack of public-sector commercial skills was also cited as a disadvantage in the PFI process, contributing to extra costs.[38] The private sector is not automatically qualified to be more efficient in everything governments do and the state can end up paying too much to secure private involvement.

Competition is the private sector's main asset in promoting productivity, but competing armies or police forces are unlikely to increase efficiency. The amount of privatisation desirable in health services is questionable. The British public/private combination works better than the Canadian public only, but the US private-based system produces services not available in the UK, albeit at much greater cost.

The method of transferring functions from public to private also needs more thought. The intent of austerity in Europe is to transfer GDP from the public to the more efficient private sector and reap the rewards of doing so. This has not happened, so austerity has been a disaster. The trashed private-sector balance sheets are preventing the private sector from funding the transfer of activities from the public sector to itself. As a result, cutting public-sector outlays is cutting GDP by an equal amount – if not more.

There is a solution to this problem, but it is not on anyone's agenda. Chapter 6 explained how a bond-for-equity swap could recapitalise banks that are currently insolvent. The same technique on a grander scale could restore solvency to insolvent governments. They would create companies to hold assets, such as sovereign corporations, revenue-producing properties and non-revenue-producing infrastructure endowed with either a guaranteed income or rights to charge users in exchange for operating and maintaining the facilities to an agreed standard. Sovereign debt bondholders would then exchange their bonds for shares in these companies. As in bank debt for equity swaps, such equity would offer better long-term prospects than sovereign debt in Greece, Portugal, Ireland, Italy and Spain.

For example, Greece is trying to raise €23 billion in asset sales to satisfy the troika of the European Commission, IMF and ECB, but is unlikely to realise that sum in what amounts to a fire sale. By contrast, Greece should be able to eliminate a significant multiple of that €23 billion of outstanding debt in a debt-for-equity swap. Recovery on debt maturing in more than a few months would be minimal, but the debt-for-equity swap would put many of the shares into private ownership, which would probably reduce the bloated government payroll – immediately increasing the value of the shares and their prospects for long-term growth.

Debt-for-equity swaps could accomplish a significant part of the required debt reduction and downsizing of many governments. This chapter has explained the restructuring that is necessary to promote sustainable recovery in developed nations. The next chapter will look at emerging countries that can assist that recovery.

11

Emerging market locomotives

As discussed in Chapter 7, the euro zone currently faces a similar style of financial crisis to that experienced by several major emerging markets (EMs) over the past 20 years. The broad lessons learned from their experience – limiting foreign-currency-denominated debt, avoiding excessive current-account deficits, maintaining adequate foreign-currency reserves and greater banking oversight – have helped place some of these markets in a strong position to weather the current financial crisis. Indeed, excess application of these principles – especially in Asia – contributed to the current crises via the global savings glut.

The accumulation of savings in Asia and Germany would unwind as Europe deals with the breakdown of the euro and bad debts are written down. With the euro in existential crisis and contagion spreading to other economies, Asian export-led econo-mies would no longer be able to rely on developed market final demand to drive growth. Reserve accumulation would reverse as exports shrink. Just as the 2008–09 US Minsky moment has put its corporate sector in a good position to grow in the recovery, emerging markets' history of crises mean some of these, too, are in a good position to invest and expand post-euro.

While the developing markets (DMs) are struggling to cope

with the consequences of their pre-2007 credit binge, the outlook for many EMs is much better. Without the debt overhang of the DMs, and with scope to stimulate domestic activity using conventional policy approaches, some EMs would come through the fallout from a European banking crisis relatively unscathed. The transmission mechanism from a euro break-up, assuming it was to happen, would affect EMs through their varying dependence on world trade and world financing. Relatively closed economies with limited external debt obligations should be least affected.

Chapter 3 introduced the tailwinds that have turned into the headwinds for recovery that plague much of the developed world. For some EMs, however, the tailwinds are still blowing, lending hope that these markets would be one of the engines of growth in the recovery, alongside the US corporate sector. Leaving out 'an end to war-related spending', which has played an important historic role but is not germane in this case, these tailwinds are:

- positive demographics;
- looser monetary policy;
- technology;
- devaluation;
- exports;
- healthy private-sector balance sheets.

Positive demographics

While the DMs are suffering from worsening demographics and shrinking populations, the case is quite the opposite for some EMs. India, South Africa, Mexico, Indonesia, Turkey and Brazil have more than 25% of their population between the ages of 0 and 14, and less than 10% above the age of 65. China, South Korea,

Figure 21   **EM population distribution**
        % of total

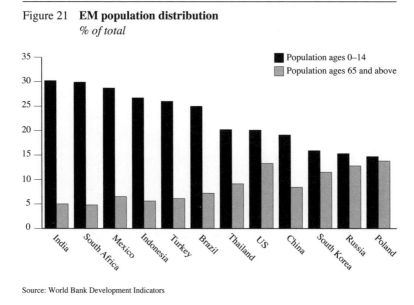

Source: World Bank Development Indicators

Russia and Poland have less favourable demographics than the US (see Figure 21).

Looser monetary policy

While the DMs have limited scope to lower interest rates, having exhausted both conventional and unconventional routes of monetary stimulus, high nominal interest rates in many EMs mean there is plenty of room to cut rates aggressively in the case of a worsening European crisis. Indeed, some central banks relished the opportunity to aggressively decrease the interest rates they set in 2011 and 2012, in an attempt to stimulate investment while casting off the legacy of past inflationary periods (see Figure 22).

Figure 22   **EM interest rates set by central bank**
%

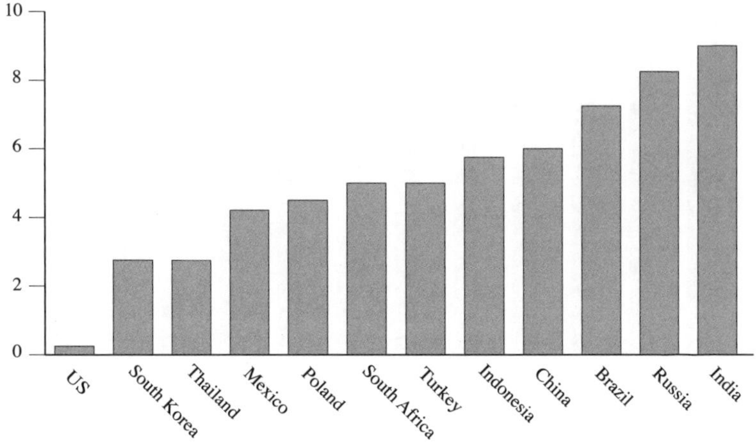

Source: Datastream

Technology

Adoption of new technologies will give EMs the opportunity to
raise economic productivity, efficiency and, indeed, quality of life
– for example, the use of generic medicines provides access to
otherwise expensive, patent-protected treatments. Asia is leading
the field among EMs in terms of technological advancement.
Some Asian economies export more high-technology products
than the US, as a proportion of total exports (see Figure 23).
South Korea has a similar number of workers in research and
development as the US (4,700 per million people). Russia has
3,300 per million, followed by Poland (1,600 per million) and
China (1,100 per million). Mexico and Thailand have the lowest
ratio of the markets considered here, at less than 350 per million
of population.

Figure 23 **EM high-technology exports**
% of manufactured exports

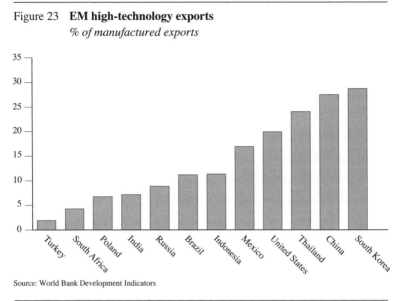

Source: World Bank Development Indicators

There is also plenty of room for catch-up in terms of technological infrastructure. South Korea, arguably already 'emerged', has more fixed broadband internet subscribers (per 100 people) than the US, 35 versus 27, while South Africa has only 1.5 and India and Indonesia have less than 1 per 100. More generally, some EMs still have great scope for further urbanisation. In the US, the urban population is 82% of the total. Among the EMs considered here, only Brazil has a higher ratio than the US (86.5%). China's ratio is 45%, while India's is the lowest at 30%.

Devaluation

Freely floating exchange rates can cushion the impact of slow global demand as investor risk appetite weakens. Several EMs were forced to abandon overvalued exchange rates years ago:

East Asian economies and Russia in 1998, Mexico in 1994, Brazil in 1999 and 2002, and Turkey in 2001. The authorities are often still willing to intervene in the foreign-exchange markets to slow sudden currency depreciation and limit its effect on inflation, however. China's peg to the dollar and Hong Kong's currency board are the two major exceptions to the prevalence of floating regimes (albeit 'managed' by the authorities to some extent).

Making full use of currency flexibility and looser monetary policy requires a sound financial position. For markets where governments, banks or the private sector have taken on large external obligations, lured by lower international interest rates, such as in central and eastern Europe, currency depreciation can be more of a threat than a blessing. Large foreign borrowing requires defensive monetary policy tightening to prevent a falling currency from greatly increasing the cost of servicing foreign debt outstanding. These countries would be the most likely to suffer as Europe works through its financial crisis.

The benefits of monetary policy manoeuvrability and currency flexibility are undermined in some markets by underinvestment stemming from a lack of domestic savings (see Figure 24). Incipient inflationary pressures can limit the room for lower interest rates and undermine the benefits of a depreciating currency when global risk appetite is weak. Rising domestic demand can often quickly lead to a pick-up in inflationary pressures in some EMs. In Brazil, a history of underinvestment, low domestic savings and slow productivity growth has kept a lid on the economy's trend rate of growth.

Past hyperinflationary periods also mean inflation expectations are still loosely anchored and wage indexation is common. Improvements in economic activity combined with limited spare

Figure 24 **EM gross domestic savings**
       % of GDP

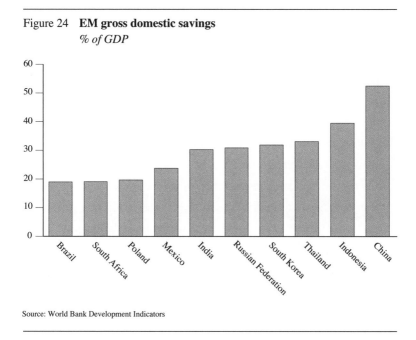

Source: World Bank Development Indicators

capacity can quickly lead to rising inflation and higher wage demands. Policymakers slashed the policy rate in late 2011 and 2012 (from 12.5% to 7.25%), but it remains high in comparative terms and the impact on the real economy was stifled by a dysfunctional banking system with wide lending spreads. In India, infrastructure problems, supply bottlenecks and too-loose fiscal policy also restricted the ability of policymakers to aggressively ease monetary policy in 2012.

Exports

Recovery should start in the DMs when exports are growing faster than imports and investment is rising. It is the EMs that can provide the demand for this to happen. Some EM economies

Figure 25 **EM exports of goods and services**
        % of GDP

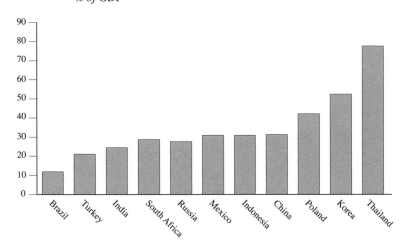

Source: World Bank Development Indicators

Figure 26 **EM merchandise exports to high-income economies**
        % of total merchandise exports

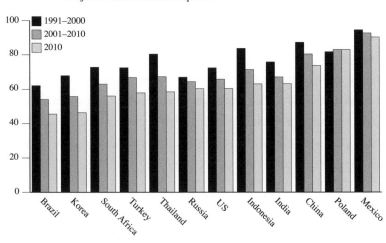

Source: World Bank Development Indicators

Figure 27   **EM merchandise imports from high-income economies**
% of total merchandise imports

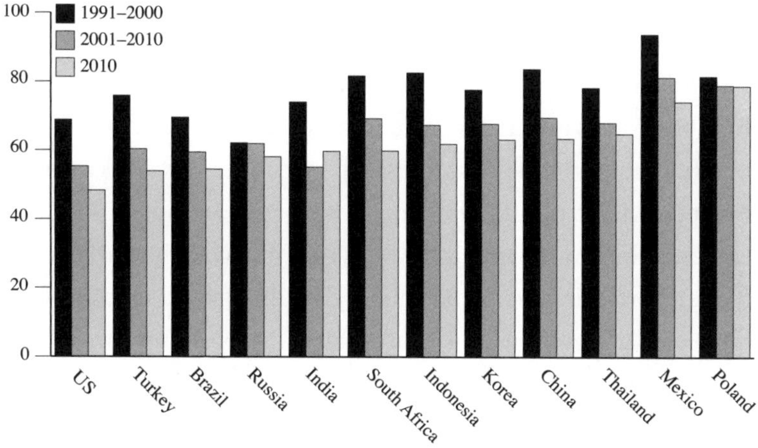

Source: World Bank Development Indicators

are largely dependent on domestic demand for growth and have become less and less dependent on highly developed economies as a source of demand for their exports (see Figure 25). Although Mexico appears highly dependent on high-income-economy demand for exports, total exports are only around 30% of GDP. Less than 60% of Brazil's exports go to high-income economies, and total exports are only 12% of GDP. Less good news is that imports from highly developed economies are also on the decline (see Figures 26 and 27).

Export shares of GDP can be deceptive, however. On the face of it, Brazil should be relatively insulated from a global downturn on the basis of exports as a percentage of GDP, but China's 2012 hard landing still took its toll on growth. Slowing external demand and lower commodity prices can transmit strongly to business confidence and investment, outweighing the benefits of robust domestic demand and a strong labour market.

Healthy private-sector balance sheets

EM private sectors, on the whole, are far less reliant on debt to fund their activities than DM corporations. EMs do not face the painful debt write-downs necessary in Europe. Credit remains a low percentage of GDP in many. Mortgages are not widespread and corporate borrowing is low. Less-developed debt markets and higher borrowing costs, boosted by bouts of high inflation and higher risk premiums, have prevented the build-up of a credit overhang in recent decades. The aggregate corporate debt burden is around 25% less for listed EM companies than DM ones; net debt is 1.4 times earnings before interest, taxes, depreciation

Figure 28   **EM firms using banks to finance investment**

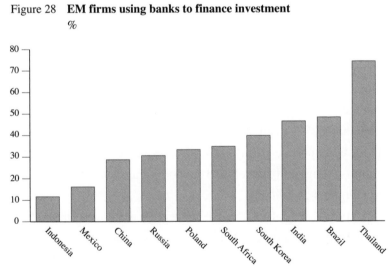

Source: World Bank Development Indicators 2011

and amortisation for EMs compared with 2.1 times for DMs. As a result, some EM banking sectors have substantial scope for further, steady asset growth.

The dependence of EM private sectors on bank credit varies widely. In Thailand, for example, almost 80% of firms use some form of bank finance to fund investment, but the ratio is as low as 10% in Indonesia (see Figure 28). The ratio for China is somewhat deceptive, as the last World Bank data point is for 2003. Government efforts to push loans onto the corporate sector as a means of stimulating the economy mean the actual ratio would be substantially greater in 2012. The ratio for Brazil is surprisingly high, given the wide corporate lending spreads in that market and expensive loan rates.

EM equity markets comprise a smaller share of GDP than

Figure 29   **EM US dollar corporate bonds outstanding**
                % of GDP

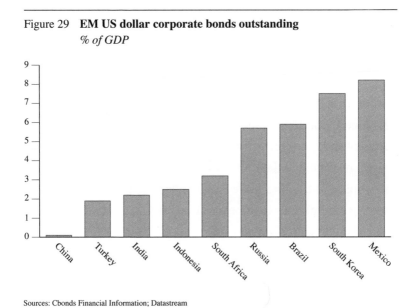

Sources: Cbonds Financial Information; Datastream

Figure 30 **EM domestic credit to private sector**
% of GDP

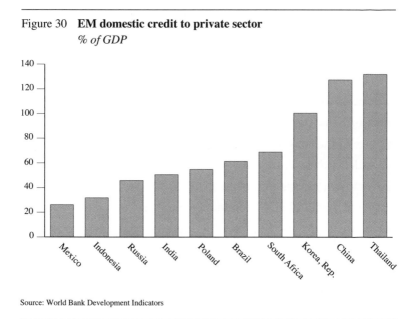

Source: World Bank Development Indicators

those in the DMs. Domestic market capitalisation is in the 30–50% of GDP range across the EM regions, compared with 70% for high-income OECD markets. South Africa is the exception, with market capitalisation of over 200% of GDP. Underdeveloped bond markets also reflect banks' dependence on deposits and short-term funding. In Brazil, for example, banks remain restricted in their ability to issue longer-term debt. External wholesale funding leaves some markets, for example South Korea, vulnerable to disruption in international capital markets and currency depreciation.

Better EM banks

The experience of EM banks over the past decade exposes the fallacy that leverage brings better returns. EM banks as a whole have been much better able to generate profits than DM banks. The foray into complex securitisation products and the explosion in leverage to generate returns seem to have created little. Over the past five years, return on assets has remained around 1.2% for EM banks, with the exception of a dip to 0.9% during the financial crisis. For DM banks, returns have fallen to just 0.2% of total assets from 0.6% before the crisis (see Figure 31).

EM bank profit growth has not been at the expense of financial stability. Throughout the past decade, EM banks have also had persistently higher capital ratios than their DM peers, averaging

Figure 31 **Return on assets in emerging and developed markets**
%

Source: Datastream

Figure 32 **Euro zone total claims**
% of EM domestic banking sector's total assets

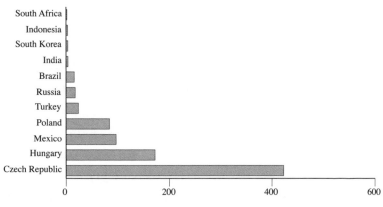

Source: BIS Consolidated Banking Statistics

around 7% of shareholders' equity to total assets, compared with less than 5% for DMs. In this simple comparison, higher levels of equity capital by no means restrict banks' ability to generate profits, and neither does lower leverage – EM banks are currently 14 times leveraged, compared with 19 for DMs. The picture is by no means rosy for all EM banking sectors, however. The underlying asset quality and future profitability of China's banking system is the most obvious threat, while excess reliance on foreign wholesale funding and a persistent non-performing loan problem are issues for South Korea's banks.

Financial pressures in the euro area – not least capital-raising plans by banks – could translate into monetary pressures in some EMs, via asset sales or the withdrawal of credit lines. Indeed, there is a risk that in their desperation to lift capital ratios, euro-zone banks would shed their most favourable EM assets, while retaining poorer-quality European assets for which there are few buyers. Exposure among EMs is varied, with central and eastern Europe the most vulnerable. By contrast, several other EMs are not at all dependent on euro-zone financing. Figure 32 shows the claims of the euro zone on several EM markets, across the public, private and financial sectors, as a percentage of total assets of the domestic banking systems. This gives a sense of the scale of the presence of foreign banks in the funding of these economies, relative to the size of domestic financial sectors.

While DM governments have become beholden to their over-large banking sectors, many EM banking systems do not have a too-big-to-fail category, where institutional failure would cause collateral damage to the economy. The total assets of UK banks were almost ten times larger than UK GDP in 2011, whereas the

Figure 33 **EM banking sector total assets**
% of GDP

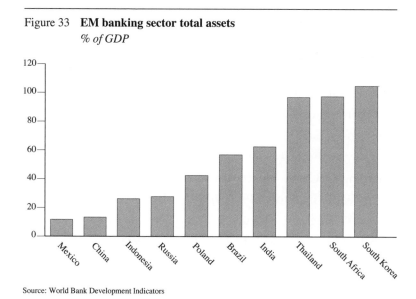

Source: World Bank Development Indicators

total assets of publicly listed EM banks were only a small portion of national GDP (see Figure 33).

China's Minsky cycle more advanced

Generalisations about EMs are fraught with hazard, not least given China's unique position. Indeed, China may be the location of the third Minsky moment of the 21st century. While leverage levels are in general low across the EMs, many have already moved to the speculative stage of the Minsky cycle and China may have already crossed the bridge to Ponzi. Private-sector credit growth has reached elevated levels in several other major EMs – Brazil, Turkey and Russia, in particular. The stock of debt is generally low (see Figure 30), but rates of default can be high. In Brazil, non-performing loan ratios on individual lending are as high as 14%. Officially reported non-performing loan figures by the Chinese banks are likely to wildly overstate the quality of their loan books. Before its IPO (initial public offering) in 2008, 24% of Agricultural Bank of China's loan book was classed as non-performing. The authorities took the bulk of these bad loans in return for equity, driving the ratio down to 4%.

There are already signs of speculative/Ponzi-style financing emerging in China. Negative real deposit rates have increased the appeal to investors of so-called WMPs (wealth management products) – higher-yielding fixed-term deposits backed by assets. The ability to move the WMPs off balance sheet appeals to banks subject to tough reserve requirements. Some of these products are reportedly backed by highly illiquid and questionable real-estate assets and new funds are needed to pay maturing deposits.[39] It is highly likely that China's banks will need to be recapitalised as the economy transitions from an investment-led to a consumption-led one, not least if unprofitable enterprises are allowed to fail, but the Chinese state has enough capacity to carry out this recapitalisation if necessary and has, indeed, done so before.

Even though China has obvious problems, trend growth of 5% in the world's second-largest economy offers significant export potential to the much slower growing developed countries. Chinese policies to reduce dependence on investment and exports for growth and stimulate domestic demand have been raising household incomes much faster than GDP. As a result, imports have been growing much faster than exports. The differentials will narrow, but Chinese imports will be a positive factor for developed country growth for many years. DM producers of cars and luxury goods have already benefited in recent years from increasing affluence among some Chinese consumers. Unlocking domestic savings through reform of the social security system and opening the capital account ought to drive further consumption growth and, with it, demand for imports.

Emerging markets can lead the recovery

Emerging markets with low government and private debt levels, healthy banking systems and domestic-focused economies could pass through the euro-zone debt crisis with no more than a cyclical slowdown. Even markedly slower rates of growth in the EMs should outpace performance in the US and euro zone over the next few years. Markets closely dependent on export demand from China would suffer most as the regional locomotive undergoes the shift from investment and export-led growth to a consumption-driven economy.

This raises questions about growth prospects in South Korea and Taiwan in particular, but domestic-demand-driven India and Indonesia should be far more insulated. China's hard landing and rebalancing are likely to drive trend growth down from past rates of around 10% a year to 5%, according to Lombard Street Research estimates. India and Turkey need lower rates of growth to 'dry out', but they are starting from still-high rates of 7% to 8%. While a growth rate of 5% for India would be considered fairly abysmal, it is still many times better than what the US and euro zone can expect. Even slow-growing EMs, such as Poland and South Africa, are still managing to expand GDP in the 3–4% range.

Commodity-price dependence could be the Achilles heel for some emerging markets. A euro-zone debt restructuring and ensuing recession could weigh heavily on some commodities, especially those with large futures markets, such as oil and industrial metals. This would support economies heavily dependent on commodity imports and help to reduce headline inflation in the EMs. Cheaper fuel imports would be of benefit to India in particular, where fuel comprises around one-third of merchandise inputs, and end-user subsidies when oil prices are high are a strain on the public finances.

Commodity-dependent Russia would suffer, however. Total natural resource rents (the difference between the market value of the commodity and its cost of extraction) are 19% of GDP in Russia. Mexico has the next-largest abundance of natural resources on its doorstep, but is some way behind with rents at only 7% of GDP, while the remaining EMs discussed here range between 2% and 5%. South Korea, Poland and Turkey have natural resource rents of less than 1% of GDP.

The challenge for many EMs, post-crisis, would be whether they could take advantage of their relative strength and exploit profitable investment opportunities. Stable EMs are still at the hedge/speculative stage of the Minsky cycle, with scope for plenty of future growth. There is certainly room for capital-market expansion in most of these markets and further extension of credit to the private sector, but domestic savings are scarce in many. While euro-zone banks would be struggling with the fallout of the euro currency break-up, EM banks should be able to take advantage of profitable lending opportunities at home and abroad. Corporations with low debt burdens can take advantage of domestic growth, even if export markets are struggling with recession.

Brazil, Mexico, Poland, South Africa, Indonesia and India would seem to fit the criteria for achieving sustainable growth over the longer term. Exports constitute around 40% or less of GDP in these countries (see Figure 25), and growth is not dependent on ever-expanding global market share, unlike in China and South Korea. Their banking sectors are small and stable relative to GDP. Their current accounts are largely in surplus, or deficits are easily covered by stable inflows of foreign direct investment (FDI), with the exception of Poland and South Africa. Turkey is ruled out of the group by its vulnerability to international financial disruption via a large current-account deficit; its 2011 current-account deficit of almost 10% of GDP was accompanied by FDI inflows of only 2%. Poland and South Africa's current-account deficits are not fully covered by stable FDI inflows, but their deficits are not particularly large (3–4% of GDP).

This is not to say that these markets are without short-term vulnerabilities: for Poland, proximity to the euro zone and foreign-exchange-denominated private-sector debt, along with weak demographics by EM standards; for India, persistent inflationary pressure; for South Africa and Brazil, commodity exports to China. On the whole, however, each economy is at the early stages of the Minsky cycle with a largely domestic-demand-driven economy. Consumption and GDP should continue to expand, providing one source of demand for the devalued and restructured euro zone in a post-euro recovery.

The euro-zone break-up and restructuring should break the loop of recycling money within the euro zone, whereby Germany lends the periphery countries the funds to buy its goods. A similar change should occur between the US and China, as the latter rebalances towards a more consumption-driven economy, allows the exchange rate more flexibility and opens the capital account.

With US multinationals sitting on piles of unused cash and receiving a low return on investment at home, the attraction of high rates of return on investment in an economy such as Brazil could prove tempting in the recovery. Indeed, a shrinking US corporate surplus and smaller current-account and government deficits point to greater capital outflows from the US over time. Savings-poor, stable, high-yielding EMs would seem to be the likely recipients. Capital should flow from the low-yield US to high-yield EMs, whose domestic momentum could provide a source of demand for DM exports.

This chapter has shown that economic and financial conditions in many important EMs are far stronger than in DMs, so the EMs could help to drag the DMs out of the downswing caused by a badly mishandled European crisis. The next chapter will delve into ramifications for financial and commodities markets.

12

The post-crash world

Failure to enact meaningful bank reform could bring about a European sovereign debt/banking crisis that would ultimately cause more volatility and losses in financial markets than the Lehman/AIG default. Previous chapters have shown that extraordinarily aggressive monetary and fiscal policies postponed the deflation that occurs when credit bubbles burst – at the great cost of neutering monetary policy and trashing public income statements and balance sheets. Little is left to ease the pain of a European crisis. The timing of such a crisis is unpredictable, so wise investors are accumulating a substantial store of liquidity to pick up the resulting bargains when they appear.

Only extremely liquid short-term investments will provide the needed liquidity because sovereign and central bank balance sheets are in a much worse condition than in the Lehman/AIG default, so the ability to offset the deflationary effects of the crisis has been severely compromised. As a result, the crisis would cause massive deleverage, which, in turn, would cause a severe liquidity squeeze that would produce the bargains of a lifetime. The most liquid investments are short US Treasury bonds. The US is not AAA credit rated but, in the real world, nor is any other country. The US has the largest and most advanced economy, and is rapidly developing a big advantage over the rest of the world with the lowest cost of energy – and not only in oil and gas. The rate of increase of solar power generation has gone parabolic because costs per kilowatt-hour are becoming competitive with natural gas.

The US banking system is also better capitalised than most, but the most important reason to hold Treasuries is that deleverage due to the crisis will be positive for the dollar. The dollar is by far the most borrowed currency. BIS statistics show that half of all dollar-denominated bank assets do not involve a US counterparty, so non-US borrowing from non-US banks for domestic purposes accounts for half of all dollar borrowing. Foreign borrowers immediately convert the dollars into the national currency. The dollars end up in the central bank, which uses them to buy dollar-denominated securities. This puts dollars unrelated to US trade and investment flows into global financial markets, depressing the dollar's foreign-exchange value.

Borrowers must buy dollars to repay their loans, which ultimately come from the central banks' liquidating of dollar assets in global markets, putting upward pressure on the dollar's foreign-exchange value. Borrower defaults have the same effect, as they force lenders to buy dollars to repay the liability offsetting the dollar loan. The recession and Latin American debt crisis in the early 1980s drove the major currencies' trade-weighted dollar index up by more than half from 93 to 144. Changes in the dollar have a strong negative correlation with changes in international reserves. The rise in international reserves has slowed dramatically and the liquidity squeeze from the European crisis should cause a drop in international reserves and a strong rise in the dollar, so it would be the same safe haven in the European crisis as in the Lehman/AIG default and the Latin American crisis.

The returns to non-US borrowers on dollar cash in the next couple of years should be among the best available. US borrowers and those not convinced of the strong dollar story may prefer precious metals stocks, as precious metals provide the only escape from debt-based money. Plunging real interest rates across the globe from record high savings rates and unprecedented monetary stimulus have raised the prices of assets faster than incomes and output prices for a long time. Gold is no exception.

Gold closed 2012 at a higher price for the 12th consecutive year – a new record for commodities – even though the biggest demand, jewellery, fell well below the levels attained in the credit bubble. Central banks have greatly increased confidence in gold's renaissance by reversing from big sellers up to 2007 to equally big buyers in 2011–12. The biggest (presumably the most knowledgeable) players in derivatives markets are positioned – albeit nervously – for higher precious metals prices. In addition, the use of gold as money is rising, albeit from a tiny base. Gold was widely used as collateral in the past. Talk about gold-backed bonds is increasing; the Basel Committee is studying a proposal to make gold a Tier 1 asset with a zero risk weighting; and some emerging countries are monetising gold (see Chapter 10).

Investment demand for gold doubled from 2008 to 2009 then fell for the next two years, but rising emerging market demand more than offset that drop. High inflation and negative real interest rates in India boosted gold buying, while accumulated savings and the inflation from monetary stimulus far surpassing that of any other country ignited gold fever in China. China's gold imports surpassed India's for the first time in the fourth quarter of 2011. The two countries' imports of gold rose to levels that shattered the close correlation between gold prices and investment demand that had prevailed in the credit bubble. Neither expected drops in supply nor surges in demand materialised, so supply and demand seemed to be balanced in 2012.

Gold mine equities embody a perpetual call on the price of gold. The value of that call usually raises the price of gold stocks faster than the price of the metal; but gold stock prices fell relative to gold in the three years 2010–12 because mining managements made three serious errors. First, failure to eliminate their hedges on future production for the first 10 years of the 12-year bull market to early 2013 greatly reduced profits. Second, they let operating costs spiral out of control. The marginal cost of producing gold is now $1,450 per ounce, according to James Steel of HSBC[40] – a level the price of gold first crossed in 2011. Third, some exploration and acquisition policies have been disastrous, causing substantial write-offs.

Writing off overoptimistic investment is almost complete and, for the first time in living memory, gold mine price/earnings ratios (apart from those that wrote off exploration or acquisition costs in 2012) and dividend yields are becoming competitive with market averages. Moreover, the book costs of ounces in the ground reflect the elevated costs of extraction. Gold stock prices seem to have priced in all the mismanagement. Moreover, plunging equity prices alerted management to the fact that they are in business to make money, so they have initiated shareholder-friendly actions, such as making dividends responsive to gold prices.

The price of gold seems high and its immediate outlook is poor. Both its trend rate of growth and its relationship to the US consumer price index (CPI) put it at under $1,000 per ounce. Furthermore, the looming European crisis makes gold's prospects even poorer, because it would usher in serious deleverage that would lower inflation in emerging countries and push developed countries into deflation, which would raise real interest rates. As mentioned previously, deleverage would increase the price of the dollar. Low to negative real interest rates and a weak US dollar were major factors in the explosive rise in the price of gold. The reversal of those two factors threatens to weaken the price of gold, and the price of silver would fall relative to that of gold.

Gold analysts focus on quarterly demand and supply while ignoring the aboveground supply, which may be 60 times annual output. Gold scrap has begun to have a significant impact on prices, as it accounted for a high of almost two-thirds of mine production in 2009 and 59% in the first three quarters of 2012. In addition, the gross market value of gold derivatives outstanding at the end of 2011 was little over one-third of annual demand, yet derivatives have accounted for much of the trading in gold over the years.

Gold, gold derivatives and gold mining shares should remain liquid in the liquidity squeeze from a European debt crisis. This liquidity should push their prices down, because some investors would be forced to sell them to post margin on illiquid assets. If the price of gold falls below $1,525, there is no strong resistance to further drops until the price goes below $1,000, but the $1,450 marginal cost of production would keep prices from languishing below that level for long. In addition, deflation could help miners to rationalise production, acquisition and exploration costs, and the crisis could undermine faith in fiat money, accelerating the use of gold as money and quasi money. As a result, gold should be one of the first assets to recover from the crisis panic. The perpetual call feature of gold shares should regain its value, so mining shares should outpace the metal.

Gold's long-term prospects will depend on how much the deflation from the second major banking crisis in a few years increases the public's desire for a stable currency. The ensuing deflation should highlight the abysmal performance of central banks over the preceding century, proving that only some form of convertible metallic standard can provide stable currencies. The following analysis assumes the classic gold standard is the desired model and that deflation has created enough desire for stable currencies to make monetising gold feasible in a decade.

US gold supply is 261,492,025 million ounces; US M2 is $10 trillion and the minimum reserve ratio under the gold standard was 10%; and 3% annual deflation would reduce M2 to $7.44 trillion in ten years. Assume gold is remonetised to produce 50% more reserves than the required minimum as a reflationary measure. The remonetisation price for gold would then be $744 billion divided by 261,492,025 million ounces = $2,845 times 1.5 = $4,268 per ounce, which, discounted for the ten years to the remonetisation at 7% per year, gives gold a present value of $2,170 per ounce. This is not a forecast. At best, it is a guesstimate because the outcome is subject to the many assumptions in the calculation. The reserve ratio, the period of time to remonetisation, the rate of deflation, the excess over required reserves and the discount rate may all be higher or lower than the numbers used in the calculation. In practice, some will be higher and some will be lower.

Opportunities in equity markets

Opportunities in equity markets after the euro-zone crisis recession extend far beyond gold miners. Lower commodity prices will ease the downward pressure on corporate margins from the need to cut prices in the face of falling demand. Emerging markets exiting the crisis with little more than a cyclical slowdown will create buying opportunities, particularly in US multinational corporations, early on in the crisis. EM consumer sectors already discount strong earnings performances in 2013 and consensus expectations stand to be severely disappointed as a global recession and tighter monetary conditions take the froth out of equity valuations.

Companies exposed to EM consumer demand and benefiting from lower commodity input prices will present the best opportunities. As discussed in Chapter 11, EM banks are, on the whole, better capitalised than their developed market counterparts and so should be less vulnerable to euro crisis contagion. EMs at the early stages of the Minsky cycle still have room for significant credit expansion as a percentage of GDP, which should support rapid consumption and significant profit growth for the companies that supply it. The US corporate sector, with its innovative capabilities, ample cash reserves to fund expansion and abundant cheap energy, should be in an excellent position to expand productive capabilities, renew the crumbling US infrastructure and supply the rapidly growing EM demand.

Smaller, simpler banks and higher bank funding costs after the euro credit-bubble collapse would both limit bank credit to creditworthy borrowers and raise its cost in developed countries. Even so, Chapter 9 showed that corporate America's current capital expenditures would still be fully covered by internal resources, even if the euro-zone crisis recession wipes out one-sixth of its total internal funds. Moreover, the crisis should end the era of large-scale buy-backs by US corporations, returning companies to equity-based forms of finance. The implied greater supply of equity should raise dividend yields, giving investors significantly greater returns on their investments. The panic caused by the European crisis will produce the best values in these securities.

Equities in some countries that devalued their currencies have not yet regained their pre-crisis peaks in dollar terms. Even so, some good-value equity investment opportunities could arise in peripheral states post-euro. Devaluation greatly enhances the local currency prices of equities from the resumption of domestic growth, the much greater export potential and the greatly increased profits from foreign operations when translated into the local currency. In addition, their domestic market valuation would rise by the amount of the increased net value of their foreign operations.

These increases in local currency valuations for companies with large foreign operations can be enough to result in attractive returns on dollar investments, and investors should be prepared to buy as soon as the smoke and dust from the devaluation clears. By contrast, domestic companies with large debt burdens – namely telecoms and utilities – should be avoided. Their revenues would be denominated in the domestic devalued currency. However, not only would their debt payments to foreign creditors remain in euros or appreciated core currencies, but domestic interest rates would probably rise too.

The opposite would be the case in appreciating countries. The best time to buy is probably just as speculation on the euro breaking up begins. Domestic companies would begin to rise in dollar value as soon as speculation on currency appreciation began, and this would continue after the event as they would profit from lower import costs, a drop in external debt-servicing costs and relatively low domestic interest rates. Companies with large external operations would face a reduction in market value from the lower valuation of their foreign assets and lower profits after conversion into the domestic currency. These negatives could quickly begin to reverse the rise in the dollar value due to the appreciated currency.

Derivatives have distorted commodities markets

Rapid growth in derivatives markets has driven the price of commodities above levels justified by fundamentals, but the post-euro deleveraging and restructuring should help undo much of the damage derivatives have done to the commodities markets. Speculation-driven demand for commodities has raised the cost of living for those who can ill afford it and dampened global consumption growth. The reversal of the financialisation of commodities would be a positive for the world economy. Only those who have borrowed excessively from the future by relying on commodity prices puffed up by excess leverage would bear losses.

Much ink has been spilled over what seems to be a fairly intuitive and obvious point: the explosion in the size of derivatives markets has not delivered a major increase in financial market efficiency and price discovery. Rather, it has enabled speculators to push asset prices away from their fundamental values for prolonged periods of time. Instead of small, regular market corrections, longer and larger asset-market bubbles have developed. Inadequate margin requirements have encouraged speculators to use derivatives to leverage cheaply their views on the underlying equities, bonds and commodities. The low cost of speculating has caused far too much of it.

The law of supply and demand applied to commodities until investment banks turned them into an asset class, thereby altering the dynamics of their prices. The prices of investments are subject to self-reinforcing spirals, whereby rising prices keep attracting buyers because prices are rising and falling prices encourage selling because prices are falling. Moreover, higher futures prices can create incentives to reduce production today in anticipation of higher prices tomorrow, pushing up prices today, too. Physical production not responding to higher futures market prices can greatly extend the spiral of higher prices. The BIS reported a notional amount of $3.1 trillion of commodity derivatives outstanding at the end of 2011, compared with $443 billion dollars in the first half of 1998, when data collection began. In 2008, oil and agricultural commodity prices, initially supported by tight supply conditions, spiralled to historic highs and were only brought back down to earth by the US subprime crisis.

The argument that more derivatives contracts must lead to a more efficient allocation of resources can be traced back to the theoretical concept of 'Pareto optimality', where any changes to the allocation of resources would make at least one person worse off. This optimal equilibrium relies on several theoretical underpinnings, one of which is complete markets – a full set of derivative contracts on all possible states of the world. Clearly, no such set of derivative contracts actually exists and one would be impossible to construct, not least without perfect information – another condition needed to reach a general economic equilibrium.

While a complete set of derivative contracts might help us all to achieve an economic nirvana, a partial set of contracts can do more harm than good. Even economic theory suggests we could end up in a worse equilibrium than where we started off by trying to satisfy only some, but not all, of the equilibrium conditions. William Brock and his co-authors show that, where at least some investors base their decisions on realised returns, derivatives reduce risk and encourage investors to take bigger positions. If these are successful, other investors follow, and prices can overshoot.[41]

Policymakers are already well aware of the hidden dangers of the derivatives markets. AIG failed to understand the huge risks it took by writing insurance protection on $440 billion of bonds, most of which were secured by mortgages. Writing this insurance created a steady flow of insurance premiums, but AIG hopelessly underpriced the risk, and inability to pay the insured losses when house prices started to fall bankrupted the company. After the financial crisis, the G20 recommended that derivatives trading should be moved onto electronic trading platforms and contracts standardised. Greater reporting transparency and increased capital and margin requirements may help reduce the unseen risks in the global derivatives market, but the forces of the credit cycle will help even more.

Central banks have added fuel to the fire

Rapidly growing commodity derivatives markets have allowed trend-following investors who have no interest in taking delivery of the underlying physical product to take bullish positions on oil, corn, soybean and other commodities in recent years. Developed country central banks added fuel to the fire with widespread negative real interest rates, which made zero-yielding commodities substantially more attractive. Moreover, central banks provided speculators with more than enough liquidity to make all the bets they wanted. This, of course, is the point of quantitative easing – lowering yields and increasing liquidity to encourage investors to assume more risk, thereby raising the prices of risk assets in the hope that the artificially created wealth would trickle into the economy. The first part has worked well, as most risk asset prices are well above their lows.

However, commodities as an asset class have prevented the second part from working well. For example, Middle East tensions and logistical problems partially explain crude oil prices remaining at such high levels in 2011 and 2012, in spite of a persistent excess of global supply over demand since late 2011 – even though it was mitigated by OPEC production cuts. However, negative real interest rates and central bank liquidity were a major factor too. Oil started rallying in earnest after Ben Bernanke's 2010 Jackson Hole speech telegraphing QE2 (a second round of quantitative easing) and has never looked back. Emerging economies, where commodities tend to play a larger role in the CPI (food and energy are a relatively large proportion of consumption baskets), have been particularly vulnerable to the effect of successive rounds of QE on commodity prices – even though capital inflows, currency appreciation and domestic subsidies mitigated the impact.

Unlike most countries, the US has continued to grow near trend rates, but that growth has benefited only the elite because the rise in commodity prices has increased inflation faster than wages. As a result, poverty (measured by the increase in the number of people receiving food stamps) has soared in the recovery. Higher commodity prices, especially food, exacerbated China's hard landing and are helping to spread the depressions in peripheral EU countries to the core. Rising interest rates should soon lower commodity prices.

Look forward to cheaper commodity prices

The euro-zone collapse should cause a cyclical downswing in global growth and a widespread deleveraging in financial markets, including commodities. As a result, commodity prices should drop to levels approximating their marginal cost of production. All commodities will be affected, but this analysis will concentrate on one of the most important: energy.

Few have followed the best-practice example of Norway. It puts a significant part of its oil revenues into the Norwegian sovereign wealth fund, which invests this capital abroad. This avoids domestic overheating from excess liquidity, offsets the upward pressure on its currency from its current-account surplus, and creates an income flow to alleviate sharp and permanent decreases in oil prices and/or diminished production. Even though few are following this example, lower commodity prices for net commodity exporters would not be uniformly negative, as the resulting lower currencies would increase the potential for non-commodity exports and import substitution. However, countries that have become dependent on the highly inflated commodity prices of recent years to pay for extravagant government spending, such as Russia and some Middle Eastern countries, will face difficult times.

The supply of energy is forecast to grow steadily, but a slow post-euro restructuring recovery could constrain demand. The US already has an abundant supply of natural gas, as proven reserves increased by over 40% to 245 trillion cubic feet between 2006 and 2011. Adding in unproved other gas reserves including shale gas gives a 70% increase over the past decade. Hydraulic fracturing and horizontal drilling have revolutionised access to natural gas

Figure 34 **US natural gas supply**
trillion cubic feet

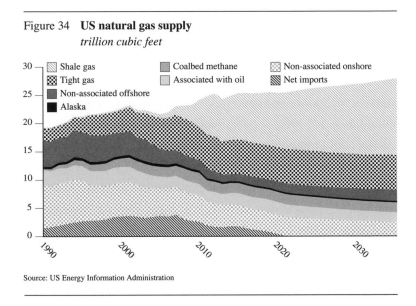

Source: US Energy Information Administration

reserves in the US and contributed to the collapse of the natural gas price since 2008. Hydraulic fracturing involves pumping high-pressure fluid into shale formations to crack the rock. Horizontal (rather than vertical) drilling requires fewer wells to access the same amount of reservoir volume.[42]

The US Energy Information Administration (EIA) expects natural gas production to increase by 29% from 2010 to 2035, almost all driven by shale gas production (see Figure 34) – and the increase could be as much as 58%. The EIA expects shale to rise from 23% of natural gas production in 2010 to 49% in 2035.

Official sector expectations vastly underestimate the potential economic gains to the US from increasing the share of natural gas in domestic energy consumption and exporting natural gas abroad. The EIA is projecting little in the way of gains in natural gas consumption over the next two decades. Consumption is projected to rise by only 10% from 2010 to 2035, with the bulk of the increase in industrial usage and electric power generation. On the most optimistic assumptions for recovery rates and extraction costs, consumption could increase by 32%, driven by a 70% increase in electrical power usage. The potential for cheap US energy to boost domestic manufacturing industry by making and using robotics has clearly escaped the bureaucratic mindset.

Even so, encouraging other uses of natural gas is one of the rare instances where judicious government intervention could be extremely productive. Burning natural gas for energy produces substantially less carbon dioxide than oil or coal, so substituting natural gas would be a quick and relatively easy way of reducing carbon emissions – as would support for investment in infrastructure to allow greater use of natural gas in vehicles throughout the OECD. At present, less than 1% of fuel stations in the US offer natural gas, and only half of these are open to the public.[43] Environmental concerns over water contamination and small earthquakes caused by fracking have tightened regulations on shale gas production everywhere, but this has not slowed a dramatic increase in production in the US in recent years.

The US is leading in the development of the infrastructure needed to export liquid natural gas (LNG) to Asia, which will be an added driver of US growth in the recovery. Shipments to Asia are expected to start by the end of 2015 when Cheniere Energy should have completed the first of four processing trains it is building in Louisiana. The whole facility is expected to be fully operational by 2018.[44]

US natural gas exports should be extremely competitive in both Europe and Asia, where gas contracts have traditionally been linked to the price of oil. The US is forecast to become a net exporter of natural gas by 2022, even on the EIA's conservative assumptions.[45] This would be a significant factor in reducing the US current-account deficits, but the tentative projections of current-account surpluses remain premature. Further exports of cheap natural gas remain a political football and President Obama has delayed a decision on further export licences. Asian governments and energy companies are also looking at more expensive LNG from Canada, which will not be available until later, because they view the country as more stable and they feel they will be more able to control the whole process from drilling to delivery.

It is not just the natural gas landscape that is changing, but oil's, too. New technologies are boosting shale oil production in North America. OPEC's *World Oil Outlook* forecast the US, Canada and Latin America to be the main drivers of oil supply growth over the next 25 years. By 2035, North American oil supply is forecast to reach 19 million barrels per day (mb/d), compared with only 12mb/d in 2010. Latin American supply is forecast to increase from 4mb/d to 7.5mb/d.

OPEC has been the major global source of oil, but supplies from non-OPEC producers are rising much faster, with the US at the forefront. Over the past decade, OPEC crude oil reserves have increased by 24% compared with the previous decade, but those in North America have risen by 43% and in Central and Southern America by 92%. World crude reserves have risen by 28% overall. As with shale gas, technological developments keep increasing the world's recoverable crude oil reserves. The number of US oil rigs has increased exponentially in recent years, from a low of 120 rigs in operation in 2002 to 1,400 at the end of 2012, more than tripling in 2010–12 alone.

Greater US energy independence will greatly reduce the strategic importance of the Middle East to the US. Unfortunately, that does not mean geopolitical tensions will ease, because water will replace oil as a focal point of discord, and the tendency for the relative prices of food to increase will offset some of the benefit that will be derived from the fall in the relative prices of energy.

This chapter has shown that in some cases the future will not be a continuation of the past. The next chapter gives a theoretical framework with which to view events as they unfold and some guidelines on how to proceed.

13

Conclusions

Chapter 10 explained that currencies that were freely convert-ible into gold automatically kept market interest rates from going too far above or too far below the natural rate. However, natural interest rates cannot be observed directly and economic models give little insight into how the global economy works in practice. As a result, supposedly independent central banks have kept interest rates far too low since the last century. Real potential global growth, which rose for two decades, is a good proxy for the real natural rate of interest. By contrast, the risk-free market interest rate has fallen over those same decades. Mone-tary stimulation after the Fed's tightening in 1996 pushed market interest rates below the natural interest rate in 1997 and the gap has tended to widen ever since. As a result, global debt has risen from $80 trillion (about one-and-a-half times GDP) to over $200 trillion (about three times GDP), giving the law of unintended consequences free rein.

Global supply has been rising faster than the demand for it, creating periodic downswings. A prime objective of monetary policy has been to nip downswings in the bud, but they are nec-essary for Schumpeter's creative destruction.[46] There are seven unintended consequences of excessively low interest rates:

1 The proliferation of zombie companies, which reduces growth by impeding creative destruction and taking market share from more productive companies.

2 Instilling false confidence in governments regarding the sustainability of their fiscal position, thus encouraging them to compound the error of excessive monetary stimulation with overly aggressive fiscal policies, which they are now trying to reverse in the face of weak private-sector activity.

3 Encouraging commercial and shadow banks to lend to unqualified borrowers. Bank risk-weighted assets halved as a percentage of GDP from 1992 to 2007 because commercial banks downplayed their traditional model of expanding their balance sheets with loans to clients and concentrated on the shadow banking model of funding collateralised assets in the repo market. This takes risky assets off their balance sheets while the banks garner big fees and huge profits from underwriting and proprietary trading. This business model change is greatly increasing systemic risk in the entire financial system. Chains of collateral rehypothecation and huge offsetting positions in CDSs and other derivatives have created immense counterparty risk. These offsets may have reduced the probability of default, but rehypothecation chains and concentration of CDS liabilities in a few institutions have multiplied the losses when defaults occur. Moreover, the international scope of these transactions means a failure could have a significant impact on foreign-exchange rates.

4 Overly pervasive central bank activity, making it virtually impossible to establish what true market pricing might be, so economic and financial analysis has become superfluous. Markets are now merely the result of consensus opinion of the timing and scope of the next central bank move, so some, such as interbank markets, are collapsing. Spread markets are also becoming less functional and

more speculative. The shadow banks' business model is even more pro-cyclical than that of the commercial banks, and their combined activities fostered enough speculation to create serial asset bubbles.

5 Ultra-low interest rates, which are hitting pension plans and life insurance companies with a double whammy by simultaneously lowering assumed receipts and raising assumed liabilities. As a result, both are struggling to perform their functions.

6 Printing money = moral hazard. Always! Excessively low interest rates benefit those close to the money-printing process, such as bankers and wealthy speculators, at the cost of the non-financial companies and workers who produce the wealth, but exist far away from the money-printing process. This is increasing income inequality and hands political power to those who are redistributing wealth from the poor to the rich, such as too-big-to-fail bankers. This is the reverse of the trickledown effect of wealth that proponents of monetary stimulation claim. This claim assumes that lower interest rates stimulate spending, but China has proven that financial repression lowers households' income share of GDP, so is not sustainable – even where growth is fast and household incomes are a relatively small share of GDP.

7 The credit that ultra-low interest rates generate in excess of saving in any given period creates overinvestment (read bad debt), for example widespread housing bubbles. Higher house prices increase the cost of housing for everyone, reducing growth in consumption and living standards until the bubble collapses. Housing bubbles have burst in some countries and soon will in others. In addition, the current cash accumulation on non-financial corporation balance sheets is a normal response to the overinvestment induced by excessively low interest rates. Excess capacity has eliminated the need to expand, while past investment has created the huge capital consumption allowances that are augmenting cash flow.

These unintended consequences have begun to reverse the unsustainable growth and rise in asset prices they created. Bank lending rates have fallen far less than policy rates; lending standards (especially in Europe) have tightened considerably; the peaking of the growth in international foreign-exchange reserves reversed the rise in the Eurasian savings glut in the second quarter of 2011; and growth in the developed country monetary base and broad money supply is slowing. Money velocity is also slowing. These are all signs of a developing monetary squeeze in spite of the best efforts of the monetary authorities to prevent one.

The responses of financial markets to more monetary stimulation, especially the Fed's unlimited QE, have weakened significantly. This means that they have finally sussed out that the scheme of ever lower interest rates creating ever more Ponzi debt has collapsed and global growth has begun to slow, so deleverage by defaulting on debt should soon accelerate. This change has profound long-term consequences, which will require economic thought to embrace both the paradigms that have evolved over the centuries.

Two paradigms

Two different paradigms have competed for attention in the study of economics. The first looks at the ethics of production and consumption in the social context of the nation state. The men who originated the profession of economist (and all of them were men) considered the entire operation of the nation state. They were, at least in part, moral philosophers and were concerned mainly with the ethics of production and consumption.

They discussed how politics, social conditions and the ethics of the day affected the economy and vice versa. They referred to this interplay as the political economy. It was a holistic approach in all senses of the word. Adam Smith's *An Inquiry into the Nature and Causes of the Wealth of Nations*, published in 1776, became the first economics textbook. It contained no graphs, no tables and no equations. Nor did its replacement, John Stuart Mill's *Principles of Political Economy: Some of Their Applications to Social Philosophy*, published in 1848.

The third-generation textbook, Alfred Marshall's *Principles of Economics* (note the absence of the word political), published in 1890, began the transition to the second paradigm: the modern, political-free, social-free, value-free, mathematically oriented economic analysis. It had a meagre 39 charts scattered among its 788 pages. Even so, this second paradigm gained momentum slowly. The fourth-generation textbook, John Maynard Keynes's *The General Theory of Employment, Interest and Money*, published in 1936, boasted only a few graphs and equations. However, momentum into the second paradigm shifted into high gear when Paul Samuelson turned Keynes's general theory into a replica of a physics textbook with *Economics: An Introductory Analysis*, first published in 1948. It had a graph, an equation or a table on almost every other page. The political aspect – gone! The social aspect – gone! The moral aspect – gone!

Only a mathematical representation of human behaviour remained. Mathematics generated the rational expectations theory – the idea that expectations of an event will always approximate the statistical probability of that event occurring. Adopting this theory and the development of ever more sophisticated computers produced a flood of ever more intricate mathematical models of various economies. Unfortunately, the difference between the early model forecasts and the forecasts of naive observers who assumed this quarter would be just like the last quarter were, in the words of one enthusiastic model builder, 'distressingly small'. Other model builders admitted that they wouldn't need the models if they knew enough to input them correctly.

Undeterred by these minor setbacks, model builders tackled financial markets. The rational expectations theory led to the efficient markets hypothesis – that financial markets embody all available information and market participants are cognisant of said information, so only random errors made markets deviate from their equilibrium positions. Eureka! The economic and financial models could be merged and the interplay between them would produce a forecast for every economic and financial variable. And that wasn't all. Statistics had reduced risk to random error. Random error is statistically quantifiable. Not only could the outcome be predicted with decimal-point accuracy, but so too could risk.

And that still wasn't all. The models could create a never-ending supply of AAA securities out of a bunch of loans, none of which rated even close to AAA on its own. Mathematics had created a paradise – until two serpents named fat-tailed risk and correlation risk slithered into the garden. Statistical probability creates a curve shaped like a bell called, unimaginatively, a bell curve. Unfortunately for model builders, the occurrence of relatively extreme events is far greater than the tails of the bell curve predict. Worse, those more-common-than-expected extreme events not only drive the predicted variables in the reverse direction from the models' predictions, but also do so with unpredictable ferocity. The European sovereign debt/banking crisis threatens to be the mother of all fat-tailed risks.

Correlation risk is the risk that two supposedly independent variables are in fact both controlled by a third. Correlation risk caused the subprime mortgage fiasco. The default risks of the individual mortgages that were securitised were supposedly independent risks. But they were not. The risks in all of them were correlated by universally shoddy underwriting practices and by the housing bubble that burst in the middle of 2006 – before most of the defaulted loans had been made.

Mathematics turned economics into the only study of human behaviour that does not link with any other study of humankind. Empirical evidence has always contradicted the concept of rational people, and the all-knowing, ever rational *Homo sapiens* postulated in economic theory never existed and never will. But they entered mainstream thought anyway. Greed and fear trump rational expectations every time, so fat-tail events will bedevil economic, financial and risk models forever. Humans being herd animals means their activities will always be correlated.

A year or two before the AIG/Lehman Brothers bankruptcy, some people, not blindsided by mathematics, predicted that an extreme event would soon rattle economies and financial markets. The mathematicians shouted them down. This does not belittle mathematics. Mathematics is absolutely essential for economies to function properly, but it is only a tool. Use it wisely and it bestows great benefits. Use it unwisely, like endowing economic, financial and risk models with infallibility, and it becomes a weapon of mass destruction.

What to do now

As Mark Twain said, 'History doesn't repeat itself, but it does rhyme.' Chapter 1 described the evolution of credit cycles. Investors who are bearish are justified because developed countries are now in the deleverage part of the credit cycle – the worst part. And the worst part of the worst part is still in the future. Everyone should look far beyond mathematics to successfully navigate their way through the turbulent times that the AIG/Lehman default initiated in 2008. In 1928, few people forecast the Great Depression that began the next year and surely no one forecast the Second World War – even though it was a direct result of the Great Depression.

It is trite to say that we are in an era of change, but the 15–20 years from 2007 may ultimately rival that period for the amount of change that will be compressed into a relatively small amount of time. Nevertheless, there is woefully little recognition that anything significant has changed, even though:

- many economies have shown little to negative growth since 2007;
- a second banking crisis was looming large in 2013, just five years after the previous one;
- fiscal and monetary policies that worked in the past have stopped working.

Of course something significant has changed. The paradigm of treating nations and people as statistical ciphers seemed to work only because almost six decades of a continuously inflating credit bubble bailed economies and financial markets out of their mistakes. That paradigm is no longer working because the AIG/

Lehman default collapsed the credit bubble and all the king's horses and all the king's men cannot reflate it, so the euro should break up and shatter any remaining illusions that reflating the credit bubble is possible. Fortunately, we don't have to reflate and we would be better off if we stopped trying – but what to do in the meantime?

Distrust all numbers

Governments have been massaging statistics in their favour for decades. Some analysts have been trying to create numbers consistent with the old way, but whose numbers best represent current conditions? We don't know. Our thinking goes fuzzy without numbers, but they are only orders of magnitude. The important part is the pattern. Patterns are far more important than numbers, especially in difficult times. Charles Dumas's *Monthly Review* on the reasons Germany should exit the euro is an excellent demonstration of the importance of seeing the patterns the numbers are making.[47]

Adopt a broader vision

Adopt the broader vision of the old-time economists, such as Smith, Mill and Marshall. Admit that politics matters. Admit that social mood matters. Admit that ethics matter. Philosophers tried to purge ethics from their purview in the 1920s. They failed, and now the value-free approach of economists is forcing business to consult philosophers to learn something about ethics. Many of the old-time economists were well equipped to do this.

Take human behaviour into consideration

For example, in 1990 West Germany had to determine the rate at which to convert East German Ostmarks into Deutschemarks. Fair value was probably about ten Ostmarks to the Deutschemark. The rational conversion rate would have been close to fair value to give the East German economy instant access to West German markets, so it could start growing immediately. Converting at less than 5:1 would price East Germany out of West German markets – making the West subsidise the East in perpetuity – but West Germans didn't care about that. They wanted one Germany, whatever the cost.

The conversion rate averaged about 2:1. The cost to the West Germans to date has been €1.6 trillion, compared with the estimate of €60 billion. No wonder the German public is so antsy about bailing out the periphery. Such insights are invaluable to economic analysis and no amount of number crunching will produce them. Like it or not, politics matter. Politics is emotional. Social mood is emotional. Ethics is emotional. Financial markets are emotional. Economists depending entirely on rationality and mathematics are like boxers entering the ring with one hand tied behind their backs.

Look both ways

The interplay between cause and effect is a two-way street, but computer models go in one direction only – from cause to effect. For example, the state of the economy and movements in financial markets always cause the social mood and individual behaviour. The relatively new fields of behavioural economics and behavioural finance study non-rational consumer and investor behaviour. They may have tried to create models that look both ways. If so, they have not succeeded. Their models presuppose that observable facts dictate human behaviour – despite the lack of empirical proof that the flow is always in this direction.

By contrast, a few analysts, such as Robert Prechter, president of Elliott Wave International, and John R. Nofsinger, professor of finance at Washington State University, argue the opposite, that social mood dictates events, including the movement of markets and economies. The high correlation between consumer and stock-market sentiment surveys supports their case. In addition, bull markets can roar on and bear markets can plunge far past rational levels. Neither could happen if the mood of the investing public was not driving prices at the time.

Remember that difficult times present once-in-a-lifetime opportunities

Do not let the growing pall of gloom hide them. All investors know that the biggest bargains in the 20th century occurred at the bottom of the Great Depression. They were the biggest bargains because the pall of gloom then was the worst in the century. A repeat is likely in the next few years. Deleverage soon to come should create a pall of gloom thick enough to cut with a knife and bargains will abound. Be ready for them.

Look for unintended consequences

Sir Isaac Newton's third law of motion, 'To every action there is always an equal and opposite reaction', has an economic parallel in the law of unintended consequences. The fascination with mathematics has erased from our minds the fact that every deliberate action creates unintended consequences. An inviolate rule for forecasters is to forecast often because predictions are good only until the unintended consequences of recent actions appear. Every change provokes an instinctive reaction either because it disadvantages groups that push back or because its success creates an imbalance opposite to the imbalance it corrected.

As a result, all efforts to change the status quo, especially government policies, produce unintended consequences that ultimately force another change – regardless of whether the first change did or did not produce the desired result. Sometimes the unintended consequences are hard to predict. The fad of momentum investing has obscured the need to look for a strong reaction when opinion converges strongly. Contrarians are always right in the end, but they often go broke before the end arrives. Fortunately, unintended consequences are often relatively easy to see – if you are looking. Some knowledgeable people, all of whom were totally ignored, forecast that the unsuitability of some of the states included in the euro doomed it from the start. Many more have noted that the German-imposed austerity policy is counter-productive and hastening the euro's demise.

The euro is a dysfunctional currency

That demise probably is not far away because the euro has become a dysfunctional currency. Sovereign interest rates span a relatively narrow range in a properly functioning currency union. By contrast, market interest rates on sovereign bonds in the euro have ranged from negative to stratospheric. As a result, euro-zone orders are no longer universally accepted and trade is shrinking. Foreign merchants have refused to sell to some euro-zone states because they fear euro transactions will suddenly convert into a less valuable currency. This non-functionality of the currency is reducing trade, investment, output and employment. The dysfunctional euro has put some euro-zone states into depression and others are likely to follow them until the euro zone's dysfunctional banking system breaks it up – an event the ECB cannot prevent.

In 2010, bank assets in the EU were €42.9 trillion (350% of GDP) compared with €8.6 trillion (80% of GDP) in the US. Furthermore, the five biggest banks in the world and 11 of the top 20 have headquarters in the EU. The US has five banks that are too-big-to-fail, but the EU has a banking sector that is not only TBTF, but also too-big-to-save. EU banks should be more conservative than US ones because the damage they can do is so much greater. Unfortunately, the reverse is true. EU banks are much more highly levered, much more dependent on wholesale financing, continue to expand their balance sheets and have 27 different regulators. They are the clearest examples of bugs in search of windshields in financial markets today.

The ECB has done all it can to kick the European sovereign debt/ banking crisis down the road. It is prohibited from lending directly to governments and it cannot recapitalise banks, which requires saving, not lending. Six decades of increasing leverage have fostered the widespread misconception that credit can substitute for equity. The only credit even remotely similar to equity is a loan that automatically converts to equity if the borrower cannot fulfil the terms of the contract. Even then it differs from equity by requiring contractual interest payments. Equity is the only form of capital that does not involve contractual, and so enforceable, payments. Equity is the only solution to the widespread insolvency in developed countries created by 60 years of ever-increasing reliance on credit.

Saving alone creates equity. By contrast, loans from banks and central banks can only create more debt – which cannot solve the problem of too much debt. Loans to insolvent borrowers merely add to the debt that must be written off, as Greece has amply demonstrated. If Europe's fairy godmother does not wave her magic wand and turn all its bad debt into good debt, its credit structure will probably collapse from perpetually rising debt ratios. Otherwise, Greece is likely to continue sinking further into depression until it regains competitiveness. This would take a decade or two at the current rate of progress – all due to inflation in Germany. Unfortunately, the Greek economy would cease to function long before then, along with other southern European states. Austerity, (panic?) departure of foreign firms and civil insurrections are pushing them towards structural collapse and casting doubt on the viability of the ESM.

The ECB cannot buy a country's sovereign bonds until the country requests a rescue, signs a 'Memorandum' ceding fiscal sovereignty to the EC–ECB–IMF troika and the Bundestag approves the application. This should remove the applicant from the list of guarantors of ESM debt, but this, like so many other things, will probably be fudged. Only saving can recapitalise banks so, failing the debt-for-equity swap discussed in Chapter 4, the ESM must provide the money needed to recapitalise the banks of countries that have received bailouts. The ESM has no money or income of its own, so it will have to borrow it in financial markets. Unfortunately, one mega-bank failure in a peripheral state would use up most, if not all, of the ESM's borrowing authority, forcing the other peripheral states to leave the euro, devalue and recapitalise their banks in their devalued currencies.

Meanwhile, the ECB's balance sheet is the only source of money growth in Europe, as lack of capital continues to force shrinkage in European banks' balance sheets. European bank problems are a significant factor in the global slowdown because they impair not only European growth, but also the funding of development in emerging countries. Moreover, the growing emphasis on 'good' collateral is shrinking the lending ability of the global shadow banking system. The limitations on the ECB's big bazooka are likely to turn it into a squirt gun. Linking QE to a specific unemployment target has removed the Fed from active duty, so a massive liquidity squeeze lurks in the foreseeable future. A liquidity squeeze = higher interest rates. Higher interest rates would collapse the credit structure because it is so riddled with bad debt that it cannot tolerate higher interest rates. The outcome would be the 24 months of pain referred to in Chapter 7.

The European elite and pundits bleat on and on about the expense of leaving the euro because their computer models cannot pick up the far greater expense of a currency that has lost a significant part of its *raison d'être*. A dysfunctional currency guarantees dysfunctional banking systems, which, in turn, guarantee dysfunctional economies and dysfunctional governments. Some national currencies would have less value, but that is precisely what those countries need to recapitalise their banking systems and rebuild their economies. Some national currencies would appreciate, but that is precisely what those countries need to increase their productivity and living standards with cheaper imports and foreign travel.

The collapse of the euro would automatically restore European currencies to their proper parities and so eliminate chronic current-account imbalances. It would also force a comprehensive restructuring of European banking systems. The failure of one or more TBTF banks bankrupting a government or two would certainly crush the power of the bank lobby and so hasten the implementation of badly needed structural bank reform. Even if the authorities act slowly, the decimation of bank balance sheets and the new-found risk that failure would unseat the management of any bank should return banks to the high degree of risk avoidance that characterised the early post-war banks. Few insolvent banks survive, so the fear of bankruptcy can discipline banks. Unfortunately, the same is not true of governments.

Government reform

By contrast, most governments have central banks that can and do buy their bonds. Insolvency is no impediment to them, so the required restructuring of government is less certain. The profusion of sovereign defaults, tax hikes and cuts in government services and benefits is provoking considerable concern about the sustainable role of government and how to fund it. Some small, homogeneous countries such as New Zealand, Ireland and some former Soviet states have confronted this problem, restructured and downsized. The parties that did it were re-elected, so the argument that downsizing would automatically prevent re-election is spurious. The European sovereign debt/banking crisis should create a great opportunity to reform governments.

Predictions of the time required to emerge from a crisis are always too bearish and the same is true of exiting the euro. Adverse circumstances concentrate the minds of the ruling elite on pressing problems. Historically, economies have been able to emerge from devaluation and default within 24 months and there is no reason the same should not be true of exiting the euro – but that does not guarantee government reform. Unfortunately, some countries may waste a perfectly good crisis and not clean up, restructure and downsize their governments.

That is certainly not a sign of a flourishing democracy. Any developed country that does not use the coming crisis to restructure its government will succumb to the dire predictions of Lord Macaulay in the 19th century:

A democracy cannot survive as a permanent form of government. It can last only until its citizens discover that they can vote themselves largesse from the public treasury. From that moment on the majority who vote will vote for the candidates promising the greatest benefits from the public purse, with the result that democracy will always collapse from loose fiscal policies.

Most developed countries face that threat today.

The International Trade Union Conference Global Poll for 2012 asked members in 13 developed countries which of the following have the most influence on economic decisions taken by government: workers and unions; voters; small businesses; large companies; banks. The responses were 53% for banks, 29% for large companies, 7% for workers and unions, 5% for voters and 3% for small businesses.[48] These results seem to tally with the apparent relative spending by the various lobbies, so probably are reasonably close to reality. Businesses, especially banks, will keep demanding loose fiscal and monetary policies. However, as noted above, as pleasant as the short-run effects of loose monetary policy have been, the unintended consequences are now making the long-run effects very nasty.

Geopolitics matter

Good feelings and co-operation always characterise the rising phases of the credit cycle; bad feelings and conflict characterise the downward phase. The authorities appear blissfully ignorant of the fact that growth was falling during the later stages of the credit bubble and the bubble has burst, making private-sector deleverage and the consequent drop in asset prices ultimately inevitable. In addition, demographics are keeping upward pressure on the costs of the services and benefits and downward pressure on the tax base that provides them as the numbers of retirees rise and the numbers entering the labour force fall.

As a result, rising taxes and increasing chasms between people's expectations of their governments and the services and benefits those governments are delivering are creating civil unrest in several countries. The story being promoted in the liberal democracies is that the uprisings in authoritarian regimes demonstrate innate desires to reform them into liberal democracies. Facts supporting this story are lacking and the increasing unrest in the liberal democracies is undermining the story. A classic technique for dealing with domestic social unrest is diversionary foreign quarrels. The spat between China and Japan in the South China Sea probably qualifies.

China's population considers all islands within its '9 dash line', which encloses virtually all the South China Sea, as inviolate Chinese territory – even though the line has no international recognition and is contrary to existing maritime law. Joint development proposals have failed. Then Japan nationalised some Japanese-owned uninhabited islands that lay within the 9 dash line. Chinese authorities sent warships to patrol the entire area and Japan sent ships to protect its islands. Only minor incidents have occurred, but both countries may be using the quarrel to distract attention from the slowdowns occurring in their economies. The danger is that the quarrel becomes more violent than either country wants.

This quarrel is typical of the downward phase of the credit cycle. Cohesion and co-operation breakdown – a necessary step on the way from the old normal of the public sector using inflation and rising asset prices to cover its encroachment on the private sector to the new normal, whatever that may be. The most bullish outcome would be for the domestic and foreign confrontations to gradually resolve themselves in such a way that appropriate parts of GDP moved from the public to the more efficient private sector. The resulting increase in productivity could then create sustainable growth and prosperity.

By contrast, the most bearish outcome would be for the tendency towards confrontations to escalate into armed conflict and, perhaps, a third world war. The resulting destruction of life and property could cause another interregnum similar to the Dark Ages after the fall of Rome. The actual outcome will depend on the choices people make. Many countries, including the three biggest, the US, China and Japan, have reinvented their economies when most people thought they were unable to do so. Others have not.

The outcome for each country will depend on its adaptability to the changing economic and financial conditions. In general, free entrepreneurial countries have better economic and financial infrastructure and so more scope to adapt than highly regulated ones. As a result, the former should fare better than the latter, but the most important factor will be the quality of government.

Today's bloated governments evolved in an era when continuous borrowing from the future obscured myriad bad policies. Only small countries have managed to reverse some of those bad policies, and often only temporarily.

The ability to borrow from the future has ended in developed countries, so future performance will have to be much better. The established political class has amply demonstrated that it is not fit for purpose. Good governance requires individuals who are fully aware of how the policies are affecting the men and women who are producing the jobs and the goods and services ordinary citizens need and use on a daily basis. Those individuals are the ones that have founded and nurtured small and medium-sized businesses. Decisions that affect the daily lives of the populace need to be shifted from the corridors of power, where those affected are considered mere ciphers to be manipulated in the pursuit of power, to the local level where the effects on ordinary citizens matter.

Local business people are best suited to make those decisions, so improving governance means reversing the centralisation trend of the past and shifting decision-making to the lowest possible level of government. Furthermore, terms should be short and pay should not only reflect the part-time nature of most political jobs, but also dissuade people from turning politics into a career. Those who actually do treat their political tasks as a service to the community tend to make better decisions than career politicians who get a buzz from the power.

Summary

Tailwinds to growth have become headwinds and the write-down of bad debts accumulated in the post-war credit cycle can no longer be avoided. Emerging markets have gone through currency and financial crises and become stronger in the recovery. Turning a currency union into a political project has caused immense damage to euro-zone growth and democracy, and current policies are increasing the damage. Without fiscal union, the euro project will unravel. Without growth higher than interest rates, delays keep worsening the debt problem.

The Lehman/AIG bankruptcy was the US economy's Minsky moment and Europe's is fast approaching. Cleaning up private- and public-sector balance sheets is a painful process, but it is the only action that can create the conditions for sustainable growth. A euro-zone crisis would end the too-big-to-fail problem, probably with the failure of too-big-to-bail-out banks, which would free governments from the powerful bank lobby. Corporations with healthy balance sheets will be able to invest in the recovery, permitting governments to retreat from unproductive and wasteful activities. Emerging markets may escape the crisis with little more than a cyclical slowdown and some will become the new drivers of demand growth. Cautious investors with cash available on the sidelines will be able to take advantage of once-in-a-lifetime bargains in bond and equity markets.

Notes

1   The peripheral nations with debt problems are Cyprus, Greece, Ireland, Italy, Portugal and Spain.

2   The ECB serves 27 nations. Some think it is not doing all it can; others think it is doing more than it should.

3   Niall Ferguson, *Civilization: The West and the Rest*, Penguin Books, 2011.

4   http://http:// thinkprogress.org/economy/2012/07/10/.../wall-street-illegal-survey/, accessed 11 July 2012.

5   Reuters Special Report, 'How Spain dumped a bad bank on the little guy', 27 July 2012.

6   Jeffery Snider, 'Finance Now Exists For Its Own Exclusive Benefit', http://www.realclearmarkets/articles/2011/12/16/finance_now_exists_for_its_own_exclusive_benefit

7   IMF, *The Challenge of Public Pension Reform in Advanced and Emerging Economies*, 2001.

8   Robert P. Flood and Olivier Jeanne, 'An interest rate defense of a fixed exchange rate?', *Journal of International Economics* 66 (2005) pp. 471–84; Homi Kharas, Brian Pinto and Sergei Ulatov, 'An analysis of Russia's 1998 meltdown: fundamentals and market signals', *Brookings Papers on Economic Activity*, 1:2001, pp. 1–50.

9   Anne Krueger, 'A New Approach to Sovereign Debt
    Restructuring', 2002.

10 Irving Fisher, *A Statistical Relation Between Unemployment and
    Price Changes*, 1926.

11 Erica Lynne Goshen and Mark E. Schweitzer, 'The effects
    of inflation on wage adjustments in firm-level data: grease
    or sand?', working paper no. 9418, Federal Bank Reserve of
    Cleveland, January 1996.

12 'Typical US family got poorer in the past 10 years', *USA Today*,
    http://www.usatoday.com/news/nation/story/2011-09-13/census-
    householdincome/50383882

13 Eamonn Fingleton, 'The Myth of Japan's Failure', 2012 http://
    www.nytimes.com/2012/01/08/opinion/sunday/the-true-story-of-
    japans-economic-success.html?pagewanted=all

14 Ibid.

15 William J. Holstein, 'Wall Street Journal Hypes Japan's so-called
    Decline', http://www.williamjholstein.com/blogs/wall-street-
    journal-hypes-japans-so-called-decline

16 Eamonn Fingleton, op. cit.

17 http://www.elliottwave.com/ezine/ewi_independent_online_
    sample.aspx

18 'Argentina's Economic Crisis: Causes and Cures', United States
    Congress Joint Economic Committee, 2003.

19 Pablo Graf, *Policy responses to the banking crisis in Mexico*,
    Bank for International Settlements, 1999.

20 Anna Gelpern, 'Systemic banks and corporate distress from Asia
    to Argentina: What have we learned?', *International Finance* 7:1,
    2004, pp.151–168.

21 Homi Kharas et al, op. cit.

22 http://www.russiajournal.com/node/386

23 William E. Alexander, David S. Hoelscher, and Michael Fuchs,
    'Banking system restructuring in Russia', Fund/Bank Technical

Assistance Team, Conference on Post-Election Strategy, Moscow, 5–7 April, 2000 IMF.

24 Pablo Graf, op. cit.

25 Mark Billings, 'Corporate Treasury in International Business History', Business and Economic History On-Line, vol. 5, 2007; http://www.thebhc.org/publications/BEHonline/2007/billings.pdf.

26 Peter Abken, 'Commercial Paper', Federal Reserve Bank of Richmond, *Economic Review 1998*.

27 Mark Billings, op. cit.

28 Albert M. Wojnilower, 'The central role of credit crunches in recent financial history', *Brookings Papers on Economic Activity*, 2:1980, pp. 277–339.

29 'Commercial paper has troubles too', *New York Times*, 10 February 1991.

30 Marcin Kacperczyk and Philipp Schnabl, 'When safe proved risky: commercial paper during the financial crisis of 2007–2009', *Journal of Economic Perspectives*, vol. 24, no. 1, Winter 2010, pp. 29–50.

31 Peter Abken, op. cit.

32 '5.4 Million Join Disability Rolls Under Obama', 20 April 2012 http://news.investors.com/article/608418/201204200802/ssdi-disability-rolls-skyrocket-under-obama.htm?Ntt=social-security-disability

33 'Unilever sees "return to poverty" in Europe', *Daily Telegraph*, 24 February 2013 http://www.telegraph.co.uk/finance/financialcrisis/9501771/unilever-sees-return-to-poverty.html

34 'Breaking Up Banks Is Hard With Traders Hooked on Deposits', Bloomberg, 4 September 2012 http://www.bloomberg.com/news/2012–09–03/breaking-up-banks-is-hard-with-traders-hooked-on-deposits.html

35 Daron Acemoglu and James A. Robinson, *Why Nations Fail: The Origins of Power, Prosperity and Poverty*, Profile Books, 2013.

36   http://www.econlib.org/library/Enc1/NegativeIncomeTax.html

37   'U.S. Consumers Still Key to Economic Outlook', *The Market Oracle*, 1 May 2012 http://marketoracle.co.uk/Article34417.html

38   *Lessons from PFI and Other Projects*, National Audit Office, 2011.

39   Kate Mackenzie, FT Alphaville, 8 August 2012 http://ftalphaville. ft.com/blog/2012/08/08/1111011/chinese-banks-weapons-of-mass-ponzi/

40   'Gold crash on Fed tightening and euro salvation looks premature', *Daily Telegraph*, September 2006 http://www.ecb. int/events/pdf/conferences/mopo_aml/Brock_Hommes_and_ Wagener.pdf

41   William A. Brock, Carsien Harm Hommes, and Florian Oskar Ottokar Wagener, 'More hedging instruments may destabilize markets', *Journal of Economic Dynamics and Control* 33.11 (2009), pp. 1912–28.

42   *Modern Shale Gas Development in the United States: A Primer*, US Department of Energy, Office of Fossil Energy, 2009.

43   OPEC, *World Oil Outlook 2012*.

44   'Qatar looking to export US shale-based LNG to Asia', *The Australian*, 12 October 2012 http://www.theaustralian.com.au/ business/mining-energy/qatar-looking-to-export-us-shale-based-lng-to-asia/story-e6frg9df-1226494117990

45   *The U.S. Energy Future*, US Energy Information Administration, 26 April 2012 http://www.eia.gov/pressroom/presentations/ howard_04262012.pdf

46   Joseph Schumpeter, *Capitalism, Socialism and Democracy*, 1942.

47   Charles Dumas, 'Germany should not, maybe cannot, afford the euro', Lombard Street Research, 30 August 2012.

48   'State of the Union', *Globe and Mail*, 3 September 2012, page A6.

Glossary

Bank for International Settlements (BIS) – the bank for central banks, assisting them in the pursuit of monetary and financial stability and fostering international cooperation.

collateralised debt obligation (CDO) – portfolio of bonds or loans in a special-purpose entity that sells securities with varying degrees of risk and return based on the payments received from the assets in its portfolio.

collective action clause (CAC) – makes changes to the terms of a bond agreed to by the specified majority of bondholders; legally binding on all holders of the bond.

Consumer Price Index (CPI) – measures changes in the price level of consumer goods and services purchased by households.

contingent convertibles (CoCos) – bonds that automatically convert into shares if capital levels fall below a preset trigger.

credit default swap (CDS) – agreement that the CDS seller will compensate the buyer for the net loss from a predefined credit event.

derivatives – wide variety of contracts, such as CDOs, swaps, futures, options, caps, floors, collars and forwards, the value of which derives from the performance of underlying market factors, such as interest rates, currency exchange rates, commodities, equity prices and market indices.

developed market (DM) – any one of the 34 members of the Organization for Economic Co-operation and Development.

Efficient Markets Hypothesis (EMH) – asserts that prices in financial markets embody all publicly available information and instantly change to reflect new information, and therefore that consistently achieving returns above average market returns is impossible without taking greater than average risk.

Emergency Liquidity Assistance (ELA) – national central bank support to temporarily illiquid institutions and markets in exceptional circumstances on a case-by-case basis.

emerging market (EM) – nation with business activity in the process of rapid growth and industrialisation.

European Financial Stability Facility (EFSF) – temporary rescue mechanism to safeguard financial stability by providing financial assistance to euro-zone countries.

European Stability Mechanism (ESM) – international organisation in Luxembourg with a maximum lending capacity of €500 billion that provides financial assistance to euro-zone members in financial difficulty.

fiat money – paper money that achieves value only from a government's order that it be accepted as a means of payment. It is costless to produce, so governments have caused public distress throughout history by issuing too much fiat money.

fractional bank – bank that retains only a portion of its customers' deposits on hand to satisfy demands for payment, using the remainder to fund loans and investments, most of which are redeposited. This allows further lending, permitting the money supply to grow to a multiple of bank reserves.

hedging – taking an investment position, usually with derivatives, to maximise the gains or offset potential losses from an existing investment or business activity.

hedonic pricing – a means to recognise the differing utility of similar products. A computer bought today can do far more than one bought ten years ago. Hedonic pricing adjusts for such changes, so changes in the CPI, for example, incorporate the improvements in consumer utility.

initial public offering (IPO) – a company's first issuance of shares that become publicly listed.

leveraged buyout (LBO) – a combination of company management and/or outside investors, usually a private equity firm, borrows money to buy back a listed company's shares from shareholders to take it private.

LIBOR (London Interbank Offered Rate) – represents the daily average rate at which a panel of banks will lend to each other over a certain period of time, e.g. three months. Sixteen banks are members of the panel and the middle eight values are used to calculate LIBOR. This is used as a benchmark for pricing other products, such as loans. In 2012 it was discovered that some banks had knowingly altered their LIBOR reports to favour their trades or to hide stresses in the interbank market during the financial crisis.

Long-Term Refinancing Operation (LTRO) – three-year liquidity offered by the ECB to European banks against a range of collateral in December 2011 and February 2012 as part of its response to the euro-zone financial crisis.

margin call – investors who hold certain derivative contracts must post a relatively safe asset as collateral (margin) with their counterparty (usually a clearing house) to cover potential losses. If the value of the investors' position deteriorates, they are usually required to post more collateral.

mark to market – recording the value of an asset at its current market price on a company's balance sheet.

Minsky moment – the peak of the credit cycle where the funds are no longer forthcoming to service Ponzi debt.

money market funds (MMF) – supposedly low-risk US investment vehicles which invest only in AAA-rated securities and which, until the financial crisis, had never 'broken the buck' (returned less than 100 per cent of investors' initial capital).

Pareto optimality – a theoretical economic concept. The range of Pareto optimal points mark the 'Pareto frontier', along which social welfare is maximised. On the Pareto frontier, an individual in society cannot be made better off without making another individual worse off. Inside the Pareto frontier, the distribution of welfare can be improved without making anyone worse off.

perfect information – a condition of Pareto optimality where each individual has full information about all states of the world.

Ponzi – the returns from an asset are not sufficient to pay debt secured against it or investor redemptions, e.g. a Ponzi investment scheme needs new funds to pay out existing investors as their assets mature; Ponzi debt requires new investment to service interest payments on the existing debt.

price-to-book value – the ratio of a company's share price to its book value per share. The book value is the value of the company's assets as recorded on the balance sheet (i.e. not at current market prices).

quantitative easing (QE) – the purchase of assets by the central bank either from the banking sector or the non-financial private sector with newly created money.

repo – a sale and repurchase. The lender has title to the security for the term of the loan.

sovereign debt – the stock of bonds issued by governments to fund their expenditure in excess of revenues and interest payments each year.

write down – to acknowledge that an asset held by a company is worth less than its purchase price. The 'write-down' reduces the value of the asset on the balance sheet and is taken out of income for the reporting period in which it happens.

Index